PLACES OF DISCOVERY I
ASHEVILLE, NORTH CAROLINA

ASHEVILLE

PLACES OF DISCOVERY I

LOU HARSHAW

Published by Copple House Books ◆ Road's End ◆ Lakemont, Georgia 30552

Copyright © 1980
by Lou Harshaw

Standard Book Number : 0-932298-09-5

First Edition

Printed for the publisher by Copple House Printing & Binding
Lakemont, Georgia 30552

This book is dedicated to my Mother and Father

Contents

9   FOREWORD

13   CHAPTER I   Beyond the Inaccessible High Ridges

19   CHAPTER II   An Avenue of History

29   CHAPTER III   Destiny Chose John Burton

39   CHAPTER IV   In the Manner of a French Chateau

69   CHAPTER V   The Greatest Benefactor

89   CHAPTER VI   Amazing Events and Prestigious People

115   CHAPTER VII   Someone to Be Proud Of

149   CHAPTER VIII   There Are Many Heroes

157   CHAPTER IX   A Crowd of Two Thousand Watched

171   CHAPTER X   The Stone Strength of the Past

179   The Southern Highlands Research Center

180   The Ball Collection

183   Gallery of Pictures

197   Bibliography

198   Acknowledgements

199   About the Author

Cataloochee Valley in Western North Carolina. Photo by Lou Harshaw

FOREWORD

In the southern mountains, as dusk approaches, long shadows creep out along the valley floors first to surround the lush rhododendron and laurel bushes, deepening the color of the wildflowers that peek out in abundance in the ground cover. Fingers of darkness reach out to touch, at last, the tree tops. The brilliant streaks of pink, lavender and rose fade from the sky and as the day-god sun sinks from sight, even the luminous outlines of the high, rugged and rumpled mountains disappear.

Complete blackness covers the land.

Occasionally the night-god moon, pale and mysterious, will brave the mists and throw into dim relief, the majestic uneven outlines of the hills towering above. The watcher below will know the mountain giants are still there, hovering, protecting and guarding as they have for longer than man has learned to measure time.

Unquestionably, these are the oldest mountains in the world. Those knowledgeable on such things have studied their multiple layers of rock, sand and gravel, their formation and composition, and the watcher can only slightly conceive in her limited imagination the tremendous and chaotic land upheavals. Probably the first of their kind upon the surface of the new earth. From tremendous unbearable internal pressures happening, not once, but many times, stark, barren rock, and lava deposits were thrown up in masses, perhaps as high as the Rockies are now. Hundreds of firey, turbulent volcanoes created rivers of lava flowing into the cracks and crevasses. Man in his time has never witnessed such a cataclysmic experience as those that created the Rockies, the High Sierras or the Alps. It startles us to think the Great Smokies, the Blue Ridge, the Great Blacks might have been as high as these before time and the weather eroded their peaks and vegetation covered their slopes.

Time, with the sun of summer, the icy cold of winter, has taken its toll. Tall trees have stabilized the erosion. Magnificent rhododendron and laurel have covered the hillsides with incomparable beauty.

Wildflowers of tremendous variety flourish here where the chill breezes of the north are met and halted by the warm flowing winds from the south. Together they create a climate where thousands of different kinds of plants and shrubs may live and thrive together.

As centuries of erosion from the abundant free flowing waters have altered the character of the southern mountains, so have these same inaccessible, temperamental lofty monarchs altered and shaped the lives of those who ventured in to dwell in their shadows.

From the beginning, we have been a people apart and it is only in recent years that this might be slowly changing.

The watcher is both cheered and saddened by what she sees. She reads about and savors the old days

The Hot Springs Hotel built by John G. Baker. It drew many famous and wealthy people but later like so many of the large resort hotels of the time, went out of style. After sitting empty for a number of years, it burned to the ground. Photo courtesy Pack Memorial Library.

while at the same time eagerly greeting each new morning aware of the alterations she knows will inevitably come.

The most spectacular change in recent years has been the coming of the interstates. Those four lane, super highways cutting their way relentlessly into, through, and only sometimes around the high peaks, have offered visitors the first easy access to the southern mountains.

Even so, down through the years from the time of the first explorations by the white man, the Southern Appalachians have drawn many people for many reasons, reasons as varied as the colors of a hill-country sunset.

The people who come are as different as the weather, ranging from the warm Appalachian spring to the bone-chilling, wind driven snows of winter.

Their visit ranges from a day-length drive through, to as long as the rest of their lives. The pilgrims come and they find discoveries in the southern mountains more precious than the illusive gold Hernando De Soto searched for through endless days and over hundreds of weary miles.

Asheville is the centerpiece city of the mountains. It is a city of charm, of character, of distinction and tremendous variety. The now worn structures from earlier days of great elegance are still to be seen. Situated on a high plateau it is surrounded by high cresting ranges. Coming into the city from any road, any direction, the contrast of the tall buildings, sparkling in the sunlight, silhouetted against the distant foliage, are like diamonds on green velvet.

This book is about Asheville. It is not strictly a history nor for that matter is it a tourist guide. It is a book by a native-born who continues to look with stranger's eyes and marvel at the wonders of a land she loves. It is a book to share with you some of the tales that weave the tapestry of a most unusual and fascinating city and its heritage.

Ashevelle is a city with a strange and eventful past. It is a modern day marketplace of contrasts, from the used and worn to the new, rich and costly. Tall, sleek skyscrapers tower over winding alleyways that lead to tiny exotic shops.

There is excitement; there is relaxation in the differing moods of the metropolis. Intriguing sights are to be seen, interesting things are to be discovered.

It is a place where its past will forever influence its future, be that as good or as bad is it may seem.

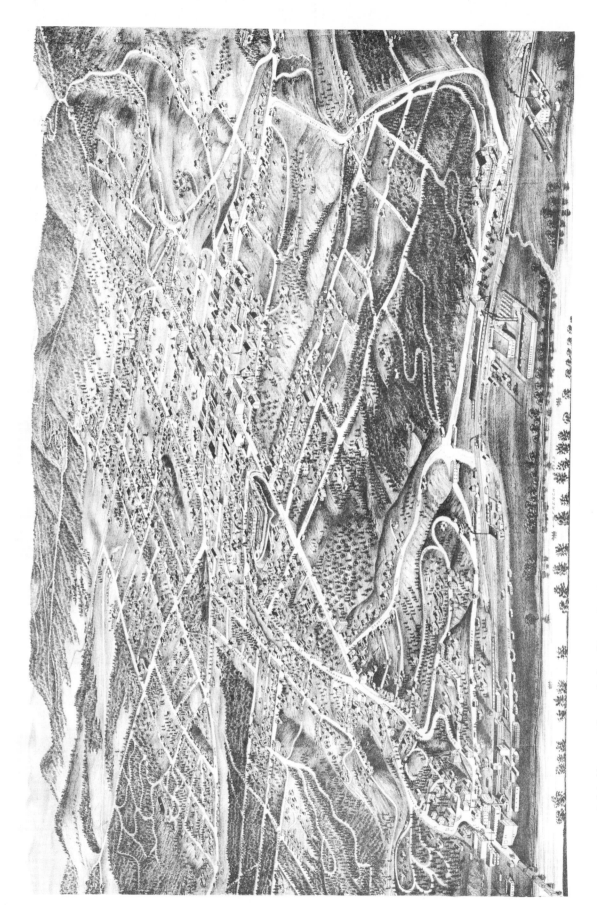

A bird's eye view of the City of Asheville in 1891. Map courtesy Mr. William O. Prescott, Asheville Federal Savings

CHAPTER I

Beyond the Inaccessible High Ridges

LATE in the year 1780, the startling realization came to the back country settlements lying west of the Blue Ridge Mountains that the colonies were indeed fighting a desperate war for independence from the British Mother County.

Up until that time, the settlers had felt little of the pressures exerted by their English overlords. These were fiercely independent men and women who had already sought refuge beyond the unacccessible high ridges.

But the siege and fall of the coastal city of Charleston, the subsequent fall of most of South Carolina to Lord Charles Cornwallis, British Commander of the South, had alarmed them. Cornwallis on the move in spite of numerous surprise attacks by small bands of the Patriots, marched north to Camden where he caught the American Army under General Horatio Gates by surprise, killing eight hundred men and taking a thousand prisoners. Cornwallis was ready for North Carolina and fully expected the state to be taken easily and quickly. He was under the illusion that Charlotte was populated mostly by Loyalists, but discovered it instead to be filled with Patriots who continued their harrassment and made life almost unbearable for him and his British soldiers. The whole town was seething in opposition.

Cornwallis, realizing that North Carolina might be a tougher situation than anticipated sent for Colonel Patrick Ferguson to join him and form a defense on the eastern side of the Blue Ridge.

Ferguson came into the now Rutherford County where he was joined by Loyalists and soldiers of fortune from the area. While the harrassment by small bands of Patriots continued, Ferguson and his men foraged at will over the countryside stealing cattle, destroying crops and, in general, laying waste to the land.

Ferguson soon learned that his seemingly easy task of subduing the back country was in no way complete. For behind the towering Blue Ridge Ferguson was told, were many well populated settlements of tough men sworn to a life of freedom and independence and willing to die for it.

Years of war and survival in Indian country had taught these pioneer men and women a kind of war Ferguson did not dream existed.

So when Ferguson sent out his "messenger," a prisoner released and sent over the mountains with an ultimatum for immediate surrender, he didn't reckon with the mood of fighters such as John Sevier, Col. Charles McDowell, Isaac Shelby, Walter Campbell and others of a like nature.

The messenger rode first to the home of John Sevier on the Nolichukey River and from there riders on fast horses were sent out over the rough terrain. The word was passed.

In the gathering dusk, on the chilly fall evening of September 25, they gathered at Sycamore Shoals on the Watauga River in what is now the state of Tennessee.

Sevier led 240 determined men, Shelby about the same number. There were 400 from Virginia under Campbell. McDowell brought his 160 "Rebels" fresh from their last skirmish in McDowell County when they had been driven over the Blue Ridge by Ferguson's men.

They came together quietly from all directions, well mounted on horses used to long rugged trails, well armed with long rifles, all of them sharp-shooters highly trained to make each and every bullet reach its mark.

They were not army men. They were dressed in the buckskin jackets of the backwoods, in the linsey-woolsey shirts made on home looms. Their breeches were made of skin also, hand rubbed to a comfortable softness. About their persons were carried whatever knives and tomahawks they could come by. These would be most useful in the kind of fighting they intended to do.

On the morning of the 26th Samuel Doak, a Presbyterian minister, offered simple prayers and while the group gathered in to head east, it was discovered that two of the men were missing. It was assumed that in short order Ferguson would hear from the two, assumed to be spies, the projected route of travel.

The men of the mountains traveled down Roaring Creek to the Toe River, passed over the site of the present town of Spruce Pine. They camped that night at Grassey Creek and by the 29th of September, they had arrived at Gillespie Gap. Here they departed from their original route, split into two contingents and came over the mountain by different trails. One group to cross the present site of Lake James to reach Quaker Meadows, the home of Colonel Joseph McDowell. The other crossing the southern end of Linville Mountain over the old Yellow Mountain road. Upon reaching Quaker Meadows, they found 350 men from Wilkes and Surry Counties under Colonel Benjamin Cleveland and Joseph Winston were waiting to join them. There was also a small force from Lincoln County under Frederick Hambright, a group of volunteers from South Carolina under James Williams and William Lacey and a few men from Georgia.

As a group, the men were mostly strong of muscle, lean of body, of Scotch-Irish descent. They were quiet spoken, dedicated to the job before them.

All were aware that a desperate battle was at hand. It would be within days, one could now possibly count the hours. But none were to be deterred. The war had come nearly to their doorsteps and they would now drive the British from their valleys, destroy their armies and remove the threat to their cherished freedom and right to govern their own homelands.

But Ferguson had heard of the gathering and was beginning to sense the strength and determination of the "overmountain men" as they were to be called in later years.

Ferguson decided to retreat.

He chose the high ground of King's Mountain to make his stand.

With Colonel William Campbell as their chosen leader and with the fastest mounted men in full pursuit the "overmountain men" reached King's Mountain just after Ferguson had firmly entrenched his troops in the accepted British fighting order on the high, flat crest.

Ferguson's stony ridge was protected by a steep descent covered with thick underbrush, trees, and large outcroppings. He no doubt felt he had chosen the perfect battle station.

The calendar had turned to October and during the night, a steady fall of rain began. In the wet darkness nine hundred men stealthily surrounded the mountain. Each was his own officer, fighting on ground ideal to their tactics. They were coming up against an equal number of soldiers, highly trained, from one of the world's most powerful nations. But the odds for all that, favored the mountain men who had put together their "army" in such a hurry. They were on home ground fighting for their lives, their families. Freedom was a personal thing.

IN MEMORY
OF
JAMES M. SMITH.
BORN 14TH JUNE 1787
DIED 18TH MAY 1856
HE WAS THE FIRST CHILD OF
WHITE PARENTAGE BORN WEST
OF THE ALLEGHANY IN THE
PRESENT STATE OF NORTHCAR
OLINA. AND HIS COURSE OF
LIFE EXHIBITED MANY QUALI
TIES WORTHEY OF IMITATION BY
ALL WHO COME AFTER HIM. HE
WAS A PATTERN OF INDUSTRY
FRUGALITY ENERGY AND ENTER-
PRISE A USEFUL CITIZEN, A
WARM FRIEND, AND AN HONEST
MAN.

In
memory of
JOHN LYON
who departed this life
Sept. 14th 1814.
Aged 49 years.

According to Dr. Foster A. Sondly this tombstone in Riverside Cemetery is the oldest tombstone bearing an inscription west of the Blue Ridge. Lyon's grave was first in the cemetery at First Presbyterian Church on Church Street, but was removed to Riverside in 1878 with Col. Allen J. Davidson and W.S. Cornell, keeper of the cemetery, bearing the expense. Friends of John Lyon in Edinburgh, Scotland, sent the tombstone to America soon after his death. Photo by Lou Harshaw

In the wet darkness, they slipped from tree to bush, noiselessly they moved up the slopes surefooted and silent. Not a limb cracked underfoot, nor a loose rock rolled.

At dawn when Ferguson came out in his distinctive uniform, he viewed with alarm the surrounding countryside. Here were the men to whom he had so lately thrown his arrogant ultimatum.

They had come and were now upon him.

The battle to conquer the mountain lasted about an hour. The Patriots advancing from tree to tree would fall back from time to time to recover and advance again. Ferguson fell from a mortal wound dead where he lay. Without a leader, the well-equipped British quickly became disorganized and then, finally surrendered. The Patriots had lost 28 men with 62 wounded, some severely enough to die later. But the British had 120 dead, 123 wounded and the rest taken prisoner.

The mountain men had accomplished what they had set out to do. The tired Western North Carolinians turned back toward the setting sun for the weary homeward journey.

They could not possibly have realized how significant their brave and valiant actions had been. They had saved not only Western North Carolina, but ultimately the entire state from falling to the British.

Had the British forces ever become entrenched in the fortress hills of the frontier, it would have been almost impossible to disgorge them. Cornwallis, never able to regain full strength, lost the cutting edge of his northward march. Later he was to fight and win at Guilford County Court House, but the battle was too dearly won. The toll of Ferguson's loss at King's Mountain, the final difficult trek over North Carolina in the dead of winter made his surrender at Yorktown inevitable.

The army that was not an army, fanned out over the mountain trails thinning their ranks as they made their way back along the Watauga River into what is now Tennessee, back up and over the Blue Ridge in smaller and smaller numbers until, one by one, they dropped away from the group to the well-known trails that ended at last at the tiny, cleared homestead with its lone cabin, or perhaps a small settlement with a house or two and maybe a trading post. Sometimes a strongly built fort for defense against the Indian raids still stood ready in a nearby field.

In 1780, when the "overmountain men" rode out to do battle at King's Mountain, the area where the Swannanoa River comes together with the French Broad was still a wilderness. Thick forests covered the high wide plateau that was a haven among the mountain ranges. From the plateau, broad deep valleys cut out to the east and west, smaller lowlands or hollows led off in other directions. It was to be four years before the first white settler was to come into this region. He could not possibly know that he would be the first on a site where a populous city would grow. He would settle on land won in earlier wars with the Cherokee Indians, accomplished at times by extremely brutal acts from both sides.

But, nevertheless, he would come, and the long march and hard fought battle at King's Mountain would make his coming as a free man, a citizen of a new country, possible.

Top of the next page—Asheville about 1900 was just emerging from its early days as a pioneer village when this photograph was taken. Dominating the hill in the center is the first Battery Park Hotel built in 1886 by Col. Franklin Coxe. It stands on the site now occupied by the Arcade Building. To the right, the building with the tallest tower is the Courthouse. It stands on the area now cleared for Pack Square. The building behind it with the small pointed tower is the old City Hall, fire station and city market. Photo courtesy Pack Memorial Library

Photo at right—This photograph was taken a year after the Civil War ended. The large house to the right center was the Roberts home with Walnut Street running along its side. Rankin Street (now Penland) crossed left to right behind the stable at the top of the photograph. Haywood Avenue followed the line of trees along the ridge in the background. House above stable is on the site of the Haywood Building. Photo courtesy Pack Memorial Library

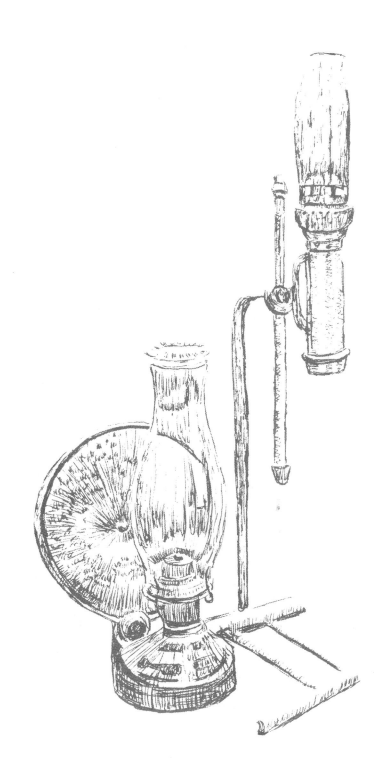

CHAPTER II

An Avenue of History

TWO broad, four-lane highways meet and come together just west of Asheville, miles and miles of smooth concrete cutting a swath 200 feet wide. For the first time in the history of this mountain locked-in land there is an easy access for travel in and out of the Southern Appalachians.

In an endless swish, the restless traffic flows by. Coming in from the east the first view of the city is through the huge cut that bisects the Beaucatcher Ridge. This new road will connect with the bypass to relieve the congestion of the old Tunnel Road, where a solid mile of motels, restaurants and a shopping mall or two are crowded together on what used to be the Hildebrand farm. The beautiful old house still stands, but now a motel hides it from view.

As one enters the city from the Beaucatcher cut, the view of the Asheville skyline is spectacular.

The broad interstate must narrow down of course, as one comes into the business section. While thoroughfares of downtown are crowded, the central city suffers, as does almost every other metropolis, from the move to the suburbs.

There are empty buildings and open spaces. At the edges where the new office buildings have gone up there is more openness, room for parking.

In the heart of the city, huddling around the large modern bank buildings are the once stylish and ornate, but now worn and sometimes decayed, structures that hold the secrets of a more elegant era. Time has flowed in and out of this metropolis leaving vestiges of every age from its humble beginning through great days of glory. A glory that was to be halted by an unfair fate before full blossom.

Even the newcomer is struck by the richness that was once a part of the city. From Pack Square where the new Akzona Building is going up, the long sweep of green park and pleasantly curving walkways lead the eye to the highly ornate city hall. On a base of pale pink Georgian marble, topped by a pink and green octagonal ziggurat roof, its spectacular Art Deco style, designed by architect Douglas Ellington, is in striking contrast to its stately neighbor, Buncombe County Courthouse. The courthouse was designed by Milburn and Hester of Washington, D.C. It is of classical brick and limestone with polished granite columns at the entrance and at the top. Its seventeen stories and massive bulk make it one of North Carolina's largest county buildings.

On the hill above, marking the southeastern corner of the Square stands Asheville's first skyscraper, the Jackson Building. Designed by architect Ronald Greene, it was constructed by real estate developer L. B. Jackson when he was only 27 years old. Its 13 stories occupy the lot that once held Thomas Wolfe's father's monument shop. The gargoyles that lean out from the twelfth floor have leered down at the moving people since the building was completed in 1924. The two story tower atop the Jackson Building once held a huge searchlight that penetrated the blue-blackness of the night sky in great sweeps, a long piercing finger of light that could be seen for miles.

The Jackson Building is flanked by the eight story Westall Building designed by architect Ronald Greene and the three story Commerce Building and the five story Legal Building, both of older vintage. The distinctive four story corner building housed the Pack Memorial Library until the construction of the new library on Haywood Street. The old library with its three story entrance arch was designed by New York library architect Edward L. Tilton in 1926. Needless to say, this old building holds many sentimental memories for a generation of school children who trooped through its doors every afternoon to browse among its stacks or hold a giggly rendezvous behind the book stacks in a far more innocent age.

The Square is changing. The new Northwestern Bank Building, the tallest structure in Western North Carolina dominates the western side. When the Akzona Building, designed by one of the country's most

A close up photograph (left) shows Asheville's sixth Courthouse when it was first constructed on the square in 1876. One of the rooms on the third floor was used for the public library for a while. This picture was made before the Square built up with the brick structures later to surround it and before the City Hall behind it was built. Photo courtesy Pack Memorial Library

In this later picture (right), with the view up Patton Avenue toward the Square, more stores have been built and the bell has been added to the top of the Courthouse. Note the unpaved streets. Photo courtesy Pack Memorial Library

distinguished architects, I.M. Pei, is completed with its new landscaping, Pack Square will enter a new life, the latest of several through which it has evolved from the town's beginning as a frontier settlement.

Asheville is a city filled with notable structures, a city that has been blessed with outstanding resident architects.

Douglas Ellington was responsible for many of Asheville's finest Art Deco buildings. As designer of the City Hall, he had originally conceived a civic center which was to include twin city hall and county courthouse buildings connected by a one story bus terminal. When the City Hall was completed, however, county officials decided they didn't like Ellington's daring design and the concept of the uniform civic center so they chose the more classic design of the Courthouse.

Ellington was disappointed, of course, but he went on to design the unusual First Baptist Church with its eye-catching and colorful tile work on the dome.

Asheville High School on McDowell Street, as conceived by Ellington, was and is a magnificent building

The year was 1902 when this crowd of thousands (right) gathered on Pack Square to greet President Theodore Roosevelt. Brick buildings have been built almost completely around the Square and the City Hall has been constructed to the east just behind the Courthouse. The Square was beginning to have a European feeling during this period. Photo courtesy Pack Memorial Library.

The village (below) is growing up around Court Square (Pack Square). This is apparently a wagon train moving out, about 1890, either to the frontier or back east to carry farm goods. The street car is already running, said to be the second oldest street car system of its kind in the country. Photo courtesy Pack Memorial Library

far ahead of its time when it opened in 1929. Other outstanding structures by Ellington include the former S & W Cafeteria downtown, the Biltmore Hospital Building in Biltmore Village and a number of residences.

As the Art Deco period continued, architect James A. Wetmore designed the downtown post office. Anthony Lord designed the *Asheville Citizen-Times* Building. In a fine example of Art Moderne, Henry Gaines designed the Coca-Cola Building on Biltmore Avenue.

The Grove Arcade building which now houses the U.S. Government Weather Records Center was originally constructed by Dr. Edwin Wiley Grove to be a concentration of shops and offices under one roof, one of the country's first downtown shopping malls. Charles N. Parker was the architect. The plans originally included a tower office building which was never completed.

Other remarkable buildings include the highly detailed Drhumor Building on the corner of Church and Patton Avenues. Its Romanesque Revival design is of brick trimmed with rock-faced limestone. The frieze which tops the first floor was carved by sculptor Fred Miles. He is said to have used the faces of local personalities, one of which resembled a merchant Cyrus T.C. Deake, owner of a florist shop on Charlotte Street. The building was designed by A.L Milton. According to an article by Susanne Brendal-Pandich published in the "North Carolina Architect" of July/August, 1978, "His client was William J. Cocke, who served in the North Carolina Assembly and as Mayor of Asheville. Cocke's father and grandfather had been members of the U.S. Congress. The site was formerly their residence and the name Drhumor comes from the family's ancestral home in Ireland." The front rounded corner which held the original entrance was topped by a crenellated turret when the building was first completed in 1895.

The beautiful Public Service Building, an eight story Spanish Romanesque office structure on Patton Avenue, was designed and completed in 1929-1930 by Beacham and La Grand, architects for the Coxe family. The building won an AIA Honor Award in 1929. Many Asheville citizens remember it as the office for many years of the Carolina Power and Light Company.

The eight story Flat Iron Building on Battery Park Avenue has long been a landmark. It was designed by Albert C. Wirth and completed in 1926. The building is in an unusual "flatiron" plan faced with limestone ashlar on two floors.

Long termed as one of the most outstanding architectural masterpieces of North Carolina, the St. Lawrence Church on Haywood Street was designed by the internationally known Rafael Guastavino in 1909. The two story Catholic Church is Spanish Baroque Revival and is noted for its vast oval tile dome, unsupported internally except at the sidewalls. The attached building is the Rectory.

Church Street is an avenue of history. The First Presbyterian Church on the left as one walks away from Patton Avenue dates from 1885. The style is Gothic Revival with a large rose window in the front. In 1951, the interior of this church was completely remodeled and the copper-sheathed spire rebuilt. Other additions were made in 1968.

Directly across the street is the large Central Methodist Church, a gable-roofed sanctuary flanked by two pinnacled towers, one short, the other tall. These are connected by a graceful loggia. A large stained glass window adorns the facade. The main building was completed in 1902, the middle structure in 1925. R.L. Hunt of Chattanooga was the architect of the original structure and the middle addition. The third addition designed by architect Bertram King was completed in 1967.

Trinity Episcopal Church, dating originally from 1912, sits on the corner lot of Church and Aston Streets. It is Tudor Gothic Revival style with a short gable roofed tower. Trinity was designed by Bertram Goodhue of Cram, Goodhue and Ferguson, noted church architects. In 1961, the parish house and hall were added.

The large Mount Zion Missionary Baptist Church on the corner of Eagle and Spruce Streets was completed in 1919 for its Black congregation and is considered an outstanding example of the Late Victorian Gothic design. The church features three towers topped by ornamental sheetmetal finials and around 30 Art Glass windows.

This church will celebrate its 100th Anniversary as a congregation this year and its minister, Dr. John White marked his 30th year of service to the church three or four years ago.

According to Dr. White and Mrs. Anna Mae Bolden of Asheville, the church was designed and constructed by James V. Miller, father of Mrs. Bolden. He was the first Black contractor in Asheville and was assisted in the church construction by his five sons, all bricklayers at the time. One of the sons, Lee Otis Miller went on in later years to become a doctor, and practiced in the Asheville area for many years.

Zebulon Baird Vance was twice governor of the state and then served in the U.S. Senate. The Vance monument on Pack Square was erected in his honor. Photo courtesy Pack Memorial Library

The Drhumor built in 1895 is one of downtown Asheville's most distinctive buildings. This photograph shows the crenellated turret which originally topped the rounded corner. The original entrance was in the rounded corner. Photo courtesy The Ball Collection, Southern Highlands Research Center, Asheville

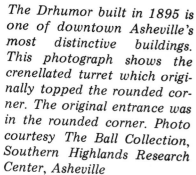

The most outstanding feature of the Drhumor Building at the corner of Patton and Church Streets is the wrap around carved frieze by sculptor Fred Miles. He was one of the sculptors brought over by George Vanderbilt to work on Biltmore House. Photo by Lou Harshaw

A smaller church originally stood on the site, before the present building was erected. Rev. J.R. Nelson was the first pastor.

The city and its suburbs contain many more handsome churches, of course. Some of these hold a decided role in the history of the area and will be mentioned in later chapters.

Perhaps the city's present most remembered landmark is the Vance Monument. The granite obelisk was erected in 1896 by Buncombe County as a memorial to Zebulon B. Vance, an Asheville attorney who twice served as North Carolina governor and as a U.S. Senator. Its cost at that time was $3,000 with the majority of the funds being donated by George W. Pack. R.S. Smith was the architect and he donated his design for the project. Before the monument was erected an elaborate fountain stood on the site.

Part of the character of the city has always been its narrow curving streets. The summertime crowds have for decades jammed the thoroughfares in and out of the city and the old tourist joke about how "Asheville paved the cow trails" might in fact have some basis. In truth, flatlanders sometimes fail to realize that our streets were laid out and built at a time when a man and his mule were the only road building "machines." It was easier to lay a road around a hill than to move it shovelful by shovelful. The narrow winding alleyways that create a labyrinth were the original main pathways in and out of the mountain village.

It's interesting to note that a walk down some of the old alleyways often leads to some of the most unusual places of business. There is a certain fascination in starting down a street and in not being able to view its length, not knowing what you might find along the way. Some of the frayed and worn buildings are being revitalized. Lexington Park on Lexington and Broadway is an old lady in a new, stylish dress.

In the Park, which contains several buildings and is being revitalized by John Lantzius of Asheville and Vancouver, with John Reid as architect, there are a variety of small shops, galleries, and a restaurant. Walkways intertwine and connect to make a pleasant stroll. More redevelopment in this section is planned.

The scene is changed now from what it was at the turn of the century when Lexington Avenue was a continual chaos, with wagons, mules, livestock of all kinds, drummers, farmers, shoppers, all crowding together in a constant traffic jam on the busy street.

The people who, down through the years, have trod first the pathways and later the sidewalks of Asheville have been a kaleidoscope of personalities. A lot of them have been nationally and internationally known. A great many have been extremely wealthy. The town has, almost from the beginning, been a peculiar mix of the sophisticated "tourists," most of whom in the early days became half resident, half guest, and the sturdy pioneer stock of the early settler families. Sometimes it was difficult for the hometown folks to realize that the friend and guest at their dinner table with whom they laughed and joked so freely, was a celebrated personality recognized by the public in New York or maybe England or Germany.

Many have come and gone to leave their mark on the city.

In its history there have been bright times and dark times. Some of these have been flamboyant, some have been sad, but all have been fascinating.

CHAPTER III

Destiny Chose John Burton

BEFORE the Revolutionary War, the Cherokee Indians roamed freely over the region.

Western North Carolina was a part of the Great Cherokee Nation which stretched through parts of South Carolina, Georgia, Tennessee, Kentucky, West Virginia, with some sections in Alabama.

Ancestors of the Cherokees were once a part of the Iroquois. A break came early when the majority of the Iroquois went north into the Great Lakes and New York region. The Cherokees spread over a more southernly region from the Great Lakes to the Ohio River. When they again came into contact with the Iroquois in southern New York there were many cultural differences in what had now become two distinct tribes. Fighting for the same lands, they were now in bitter conflict.

Also in conflict and fighting with other tribes, the Cherokees gradually moved south to take haven in the sheltering mountains of the Southern Appalachians. The rough area was perfect for their needs. Hunting grounds were plentiful, the climate agreeable. There was room for them to thrive and grow in numbers. Even so, the Cherokees had to carry on a constant watchful defense to protect their territory from the incursion of other tribes. Many fierce battles were fought between bands of red men even before the coming of the white explorers. Western North Carolina could already be termed "a dark and bloody ground" as Miss Ora Blackmun has indicated in her comprehensive history, *Western North Carolina to 1880*.

By the time the white man made his entrance into the region, the Cherokees were tough, seasoned fighters, a formidable foe.

If they were tough, they were also a highly intelligent and handsome people. In later years they were to become one of the most highly civilized of the Indian nations with a written language. They were also an agricultural people. Some of the Cherokee families in the southern sections of their nation held slaves, were thought to mine for gold in North Georgia.

In more recent archeological discoveries from one of the main excavation sites in the Swannanoa Valley on the lands of Warren Wilson College, it is known that a much earlier human culture existed in the mountains. These were wanderers, hunters. They used crude spears and had developed cooking pots. They lived in a small band in Swannanoa Valley as much as five thousand years ago, perhaps much earlier. Archeologists are beginning to believe that advanced cultures existed on the North American continent at a much earlier age than has been suspected. The mystery of Judaculla Rock in Jackson County with its hieroglyphics has yet to be deciphered. The age of the Kikwasi mound at Franklin in Macon County has yet to be determined. It remains, preserved by efforts of the local people, to prove that some ancient period, the mound builders roamed over this region.

Judaculla Rock, one of the earliest of the archaeological mysteries of the Eastern United States. Located near Cullowhee, its writings have never been deciphered but are thought to have been inscribed by ancient tribes engaged in some great battle. Photo courtesy North Carolina Department of Development, Tourist Division

Early on, as the white man settled the coastal areas, the low lands and what is now known as the Piedmont, the Blue Ridge Mountain Range rose before them as a massive barrier.

Several parties of exploration wandered into the wilderness, crossing the creeks and rivers and migration and settlement of the state began to take place. Several of them were to return to write glorious accounts of what they had seen and experienced. They were our first travel writers.

It is generally accepted that the first white family to move directly west from Pittsboro County was that of Samuel Davidson. His land grant was awarded for service during the Revolutionary War. Davidson, bringing his family, crossed the Blue Ridge in 1784 and built a cabin at the foot of Jonas Mountain.

Unfortunately, Davidson did not fare well. The Cherokees, jealous of their hunting lands, stole a bell from one of Davidson's cattle and by ringing it and moving away from the clearing, lured him away from the cabin up the mountain, shot and scalped him. His wife together with their child and a Black house servant hid from the Indians and later made their way over the mountains to the nearest fort which was on the Catawba River.

Samuel's twin brother and his sister Rachel Alexander later moved their families across the Blue Ridge to settle on grants where Bee Tree Creek joins the Swannanoa River. Soon, several other families came into the area, the Gudgers, the Foresters and several different families named Patton. The Colonel David Vance family settled in Reems Creek Valley. The John Weaver family had already come into the valley and had established a small settlement.

Zeb Vance for whom the monument on Pack Square is named became one of the state's most outstanding men. Fortunately for us, the Vance homeplace has been preserved almost precisely as it was when Vance grew up there. He was considered, even at an early age, to be precocious and headed for great things. The homeplace is maintained by the North Carolina Department of Archives and History and is open to the public.

The homeplace of Zebulon Baird Vance, Civil War Governor of North Carolina, is still preserved and maintained by the North Carolina Department of Archives and History. His family was among the first settlers in Beaverdam Valley. The house and grounds are open to the public. Photo by Lou Harshaw

Zebulon Baird Vance is buried in Riverside Cemetery at Asheville. Note the tiny Confederate flag which graces his tombstone. Photo by Lou Harshaw

Mountain Farm building in Cataloochee Valley. Photo by Dick Harshaw

Beaverdam Valley then was settled by the George Swain Family, David Killian and a little later Bedent Baird.

Another grant, closer to the present site of the city was made to Zebulon Baird, brother of Bedent, and he built a home near the French Broad River.

But destiny chose John Burton, who received several tracts on July 7, 1794, to be the holder of the one upon which the future city would be built. In all, Burton's land covered 203 acres.

The boundaries of the "Town Tract" ran roughly from Orange and Clayton Streets on the north, Charlotte and Valley Streets through the old David Millard property on the east, Carroll Avenue to the intersection of Coxe and Banks Avenues to the south, and Coxe Avenue through Pritchard Park to the intersection of Orange and Merrimon Avenue on the West.

January 1792 saw the creation of the new county of Buncombe named after Colonel Edward Buncombe. When the first courthouse was built on the high plateau that seemed to be in a central position of the new county, it put Burton in a most advantageous position. According to Ora Blackmun, in *Western North Carolina to 1880*, "The new structure faced east approximately where today Patton Avenue enters Pack Square in Asheville. John Burton, called "The Father of Asheville" from his holdings, laid out a north-south street in front of it be be known as North Main and South Main. Those streets are still in use as Broadway and Biltmore."

Along those streets Burton laid out forty-two lots and began to sell them off as the new county seat began to draw the usual number of lawmakers and others ordinarily connected with a new county government. These people required goods and services, places of trade. The first lot, no. 4, was sold to Thomas Burton for "twenty shillings." This lot was on Biltmore Avenue and was later occupied by the Earle Hotel. Burton's other real estate "deals" went to some well known pioneer families such as Thomas Foster, Zebulon and Bedent Baird, Samuel Luck, Colonel William Davidson, Patton and Erwin. James Patton, who had sold merchandise from a pack horse, was one of the first to build a permanent store building. Zebulon and Bedent Baird opened one with goods from the first wagon to reach Asheville. The wagon had been brought up over Saluda Mountain in 1793 and had to be taken apart and carried piece by piece over some of the most rugged parts of the trail. A tailoring shop was opened by Silas McDowell and then a forge. John Burton, enterprising and hardworking, owned a grist mill on Glenn's Creek, a short distance above where the mouth of the creek emptied into the French Broad River. Burton's was the first grist mill in Buncombe County. Later, Burton sold the mill to Zebulon and Bedent Baird. These two brothers were Scotsmen. Zebulon Baird was the grandfather of Zebulon Baird Vance.

The end of Burton's life is somewhat shrouded in mysteries, lost in time. After the sale of his grist mill, he moved from Asheville to Fairview and met with misfortunes in business and property losses. The date of his death is unknown.

Most of the buildings in the village were places of trade, since the shopkeepers usually had large land holdings out in the county. After a day in the store they closed up and rode or walked back along the paths to their farms.

By 1793 there was a school, opened by Robert Henry, a veteran of the Revolutionary War. He was also a lawyer and surveyor. His little school, Union Hill, was the first school in North Carolina west of the Blue Ridge Mountains.

The little cluster of wooden buildings was first called Morristown, but the name didn't last. When the town was incorporated in 1797 it was changed to Asheville in honor of Governor Samuel Ashe. In 1801 the post office was established.

There were some wagons in the region before the county was established, but not many. Most of the travel was by foot or on horseback. Goods were carried on the backs of pack horses. Roads in the rocky reaches of the hills were carved out by mule and man muscle. One of the first duties of the newly organized Buncombe County government was to build connecting wagon roads between the various valley settlements and the struggling-to-get-started town.

The first foot paths up and over the Blue Ridge could hardly be classified as roads. Traveling to and from from the east was extremely difficult and at times hazardous. Predatory animals roamed in the wilderness and there was danger from summer storms. No one ventured out in the mountains in wintertime if it possibly could be avoided.

As the village that was the county seat of Buncombe, situated near the joining of the French Broad and Swannanoa Rivers, began to spread out with more places of business and some family cabins, the need grew for a better, easier route to the east.

Perhaps the first really notable road through the Blue Ridge was the Buncombe Turnpike. It was in the 1824 session that the State Legislature passed bills for its construction. James Patton, Samuel Chunn and George Swan were directed to begin getting bids.

According to F.A. Sondley's *A History of Buncombe County, North Carolina,* "The turnpike ran from Saluda Gap by way of the present Flat Rock and Hendersonville and Murrayville (Meadows) and Arden until at the present Biltmore public school building about one mile south of the Swannanoa River it diverged a little to the northwest and reached the Swannanoa at the old Colonel John Patton place (later known as the 'Haunted House'), where had been the old Shawano Town of Swannano; and there crossing the Swannanoa River and then ascending the hill on the north and passing the site of the present St. Joseph

Academy and reaching Biltmore Avenue nearly at St. Joseph's Hospital, as those places are now called, it followed that Avenue to the Public Square in Asheville. From the Public Square, it ran with or nearly with the present highway to the city's northern termination and on to the entrance of the Burnsville Road and then followed the eastern and northern bank of the French Broad River across Beaverdam Creek, Reems Creek, Flat Creek, Ivey, and Laurel until it reached the Tennessee line at Paint Rock, making on the way a few divergencies for short distances in order to avoid river bluffs. The road was seventy-five miles in length and was considered the finest in North Carolina at that time.''

It is now famous for the hog, turkey and cattle drives that took place. The drovers moved their herds over the road, a flock of turkeys followed sometimes by a lone man, sometimes by several, with long sticks to tend the wandering birds. This traffic out of Tennessee and into the South Carolina markets led to the building of a number of inns and taverns called "stands" along the road. There were pens for the livestock, beds and meals for the travelers. This was the beginning of what grew to be a large and thriving industry of hospitality. Later it included some of the finest hotels in the country.

Sondley estimates: "Annually there passed through Asheville from one hundred and forty thousand to one hundred and sixty thousand of these hogs." The hogs could travel from eight to ten miles a day, requiring at least a week to go through the county.

When the traffic became too heavy, a second road was built from the western foot of Burnsville Hill and joining the old Warm Springs road over Beaverdam Creek and Reems Creek through the area near the present Jupiter then on to the Bend of Ivy, crossing Walnut Creek and Samuel Creek at Greeneville, Tennessee where it terminated. It was a rougher road, not as well kept nor as well maintained. Consequently, its traffic was mostly herds of mules, horses and cattle while hogs and turkeys continued to fare better on the well constructed Buncombe Turnpike.

The stage coach ran each day from Asheville to Greeneville, Tennessee. The stages carried eight passengers inside with more riding on top if necessary. Since the "stands" kept relay teams of horses, the stage by changing the teams could travel at great speed, sixty miles a day.

Soon other roads were opened into the mountain stronghold. Stage lines carried mail and passengers from Salisbury to Lincolnton and Rutherfordton through the spectacular Chimney Rock Gorge up and over Hickory Nut Gap where Sherrill's Inn was an overnight stay, then on to Asheville. The stage fare from Salisbury to Asheville was about $8-$10. Meals and lodgings usually ran about $2.50. Another was from Greenville, South Carolina by way of Saluda Gap to Asheville. A similar road was built from Morganton, North Carolina through Swannanoa Gap to the Buncombe County Seat.

The cost of road building in the Western part of the state was tremendous. As an item on the budget of the State Legislature, it was ignored or discarded whenever possible.

The general present day attitude is reversed from that of the past when the goal was to construct as many roads as possible. The new criteria is to build as few roads as possible into the wilderness, not to ruin the natural beauty, not to spoil, with man-made urban sprawl, nature's gift to the future generations.

In the downtown area the twisting streets continue to cause traffic snarls, especially in the summer months, but they also give the city a distinctive charm.

At the mid-1880's Asheville was the only incorporated village west of the crest of the Blue Ridge Mountains. The population was around 800.

The small village lay quiet in the hollow of the surrounding hills. During the Civil War while great armies fought desperate battles around and near, Asheville was involved in one small engagement fought on land near the lower end of Montford Avenue while citizens from the village gathered on the crest of Battery Porter to watch.

Unbeknownst to these same citizens, the ending of the dreadful conflict between the states would bring rapid and exhilarating change. Down in South Carolina, John C. Calhoun had ventured the theory that the mountains just to the north were the highest in the eastern part of the country. When Arnold Guyot had scientifically measured the western North Carolina peaks in 1854, his findings confirmed Calhoun's thinking.

What the residents of the pleasant little settlement didn't realize was that important men, men of wealth and power, had long been looking at the undeveloped Southern Appalachians with an eye to the future.

Asheville was approaching its first great period of expansion.

Already some of the diverse personalities which were to shape its future were being drawn to the mountains.

Round Knob Hotel and Andrews Geyser were a half-way stopping point on the railroad, up Old Fort Mountain to Swannanoa. This mainline coming into the mountains drastically changed travel in the Southern Appalachians. The geyser has been rebuilt and is a popular tourist attraction. Photo courtesy Pack Memorial Library.

CHAPTER IV

In the Manner of a French Chateau

ACCORDING to Richard Thornton, director of Asheville's Revitalization Commission: "Prior to the 1790's until the (Civil War) Reconstruction Era, the downtown was primarily wooden buildings, loosely scattered with gardens and pastures in between. The center of town was at Biltmore, Broadway and Patton where the old county courthouse stood. Many of the first streets are now alleys. Commerce Street and Carolina Lane are examples of this. At this time Asheville was a loose, rural village."

Asheville, even though still small in population, was already experiencing a brisk travel trade. In 1814 the Eagle Hotel was built on South Main Street. In 1825, the Buck Hotel was built by James M. Smith on the corner of what is now Biltmore Avenue and College Street. In a later year, 1912 to be exact, on this same site was to rise the Langren Hotel, the first building in the town supported by steel frame construction. A large multi-level parking lot now covers this site.

A stay at either the Eagle or the Buck was a decided improvement in comfort over a night's stay at one of the old drovers' stands. The stage coach came in to deliver guests at the front entrance of the Eagle every day. In fact, things were so pleasant at these early establishments that guests would quite often stay over for a day or two.

The first travelers to the mountain town were not tourists coming in for a vacation, they were businessmen or men of government. Most of the time they were just "passing through" on their way westward to claim land grants. Perhaps they were headed in the reverse direction away from the frontier territories back to the coastal areas on business and financial matters. Occasionally, however, the stage coach would bring in a whole family, traveling together to visit relatives or to seek a new life in the west.

Many did stop off to stay permanently in the little village, and it was growing.

In 1840, the first Asheville newspaper was established, the *Highland Messenger*. Another newpaper, the weekly *Pioneer* was founded in 1865 and in 1870, the forerunner of today's modern newspaper, *The Asheville Citizen* was started.

Randolph Abbott Shotwell was the founder of the *Citizen* which had its beginnings, February 3, on the second floor of a building on the corner of Northwest Pack Square, the southside of College Street and the westside of Broadway. Before the *Citizen* became settled at is present site, it was to occupy, in all, 14 different locations. Its many moves were for the most part in the interests of more space. While at one address the circulation grew from 1,800 to almost 7000. The periods of most rapid growth for the town also reflect greatly expanding circulation for this newspaper.

Shortly after its establishment, the paper moved to a new building which S.R. Chedester had erected on Patton Avenue. This was later to be the site of Bon Marche, and still later the Kress Building, now empty.

Langren Hotel, Asheville, N. C.
Completed 1912. Fire Proof. Constructed of concrete, st
iron and sandstone.

The Langren when it was completed in 1912 was the first steel frame constructed building in the city. It became a popular place for community gatherings. There was a small theatre on the roof that served as one of the first homes of the Asheville Community Theatre. Photo courtesy Pack Memorial Library

At the top of the next page is a view down Broadway (North Main Street). The large building in the background is the Langren Hotel. A parking building now occupies this site. When Asheville was a pioneer village the Buck Hotel, built in 1825 and one of Asheville's first hotels, was located on this same corner. Photo courtesy The Ball Collection, Southern Highlands Research Center, Asheville

At right, view up Patton Avenue (the street on the right; the one that veers to the left is College) showing the post office and federal building which was erected in 1892 at a cost of $90,000. In 1909 an extension was added at a cost of $64,000. The building was torn down in 1932 and the property was deeded to the city. The park was named in honor of Jeter C. Prichard, former U.S. Senator and senior judge of the U.S. Circuit Court of Appeals. Photo courtesy The Ball Collection, Southern Highlands Research Center, Asheville

The stage awaits its passengers in front of the Eagle Hotel in Asheville. Note the symbolic eagle atop the pole in front. The Eagle Hotel offered comfortable accommodations to those traveling to the mountains. Photo courtesy Pack Memorial Library

Dr. F.A. Sondley did more than perhaps any other person to collect and preserve historical materials on Asheville and Buncombe County. The Sondley Collection consisting of 34,933 volumes left in Asheville to Pack Memorial Library by Dr. F.A. Sondley who died in 1931, doubled the research materials available at the library at that time. The Asheville Library is outstanding in the scope of books, manuscripts and photographs available to its members for study. Photos courtesy Pack Memorial Library.

This was one of the early homes of The Asheville Citizen *which apparently was located on the 2nd floor and produced job printing as a sideline.* The Asheville Citizen *has served the community for over 100 years. Note the unpaved streets. The sign on the front side window reads "Mayor's Office."*
Photo courtesy Pack Memorial Library

About 1886, the paper was moved to the second floor of a building that stood on the southeast corner of Patton Avenue and Court Square (now Pack Square).

In 1887, the *Citizen* was moved again to the second floor of the Reynolds Building at 11 Patton Avenue, later to house the Charles Store (now demolished). From this building, the paper moved again to the north-side of Pack Square, its address as 10 North Court Square. The next move was a short distance of just two doors west of the old address on January 30, 1889.

In January 1897, the Citizen moved to the two story brick Carter Building, the site of the present Legal Building. Church Street was the next move in the rear of the American National Bank Building at the corner of Patton Avenue and Church Street. The paper moved in 1901 to 10 Lexington Avenue, a building which had housed a former printing company. Thirty-two Patton Avenue was the next address in the following year. This later became the entrance to the Imperial Theatre. At the Patton Avenue address, the paper occupied the basement, most of the main floor and the rear of the second floor of the building.

The *Citizen* next occupied especially designed quarters by the Coxe estate at 8 Government Street, moving on January 3, 1911. The circulation had now reached 7000 and the Sunday edition contained from 24 to 28 pages. It had become a seven day newspaper.

The *Asheville Times*, afternoon affiliation publication of the *Citizen* was founded by J.M. Johnson, his son, Fred A. Johnson and James E. Norton who had founded a newspaper originally called the *Asheville Daily Gazette*. The paper sold for five cents a copy and proclaimed itself "the only Asheville newspaper sold on railroad trains and circulated in mountain towns."

In 1903, the *Asheville Evening News* was founded by George L. Hackney and Walter D. Hildebrand. Hackney bought the *Gazette* on New Year's Eve and the following day the *Gazette-News* was published. It was to be twelve years before it became *The Times*.

Hildebrand had been editor of the *News* and now became editor of *The Gazette-News*. In 1905 Hackney sold his interests in the paper and Hildebrand became the principle owner.

The paper, which had grown and flourished, was sold February 19, 1916 to Charles A. Webb who changed its name to *The Asheville Times*.

Webb, a Democrat, sold the paper three years later to a Republican, Charles J. Harris. Harris kept it two years and resold it to Hildebrand, who, in turn sold it to D. Hiden Ramsey, P.M. Burdette and Gray Gorham.

Under their leadership it became a Democratic newspaper with a leaning toward independent news.

In September 1925, the Times was sold to Don S. Elias and Associates and Charles K. Robinson became Editor.

Meanwhile, the Citizen moved one more time from Government Street to 25 Haywood Street where it remained for 17 years until the consolidation of the two papers and the move to the present building on O. Henry Avenue.

The combined newspapers were bought out on September 23, 1953 by the Peace publishing interests of Greenville, South Carolina. Robert E. Bunnelle became publisher in the fall of 1954, and served until March 30, 1974 when he became chariman of the board of the Peace interests. Richard B. Wynne then became president and publisher of the combined newspapers.

Among the many prominent people who guided the *Citizen* over the years were R.S. Howland and Associates who owned the *Journal* at Providence, Rhode Island, and bought Sunset Mountain and thousands of acres to the east of it.

Later the *Citizen* was owned by a group of Asheville men including Julius C. Martin, an attorney who became president of the company, J.E. Rankin, Frank Carter and Judge J.D. Murphy.

In 1905, when Robert S. Jones bought a good part of the stock and joined with James H. Caine who was editor of the paper for 15 years, the newspaper began a long period of growth and prosperity.

Over the years, the two newspapers have served as chief recorders of the ever-changing parade of events. The pages on a daily basis have woven a tapestry of every human emotion, grief, joy and sometimes shock and sadness as when the "extra" was issued upon the assassination of President Kennedy. The paper's last "extra" was issued July 19, 1967, when a commercial airliner crashed at the Asheville-Hendersonville airport. The newspaper has not only served as recorder, but has been a prime mover through its editorial pages in the development of the city. It has served as a reminder of public responsibilities, a pointer of directions.

By 1879 the population of the town had grown to 2,600.

It was in that same year that a few community-minded women of the town conceived the idea of starting a circulating library. They contacted neighbors, friends, managing to get together some sixty books.

When it proved to be well received, they formed the Asheville Library Association. At first the library had no permanent home, moving from one place to another in rooms over stores. In 1890, the books were housed in a building which later became the Y.M.C.A. Later a question arose as to whether the Presbyterian Church actually owned a small adjoining lot which had been a cemetery, but from which the bodies had been removed to the city cemetery.

The heirs-in-law of James Patton seemed to be the only clear title holders to the property, since his family had deeded it to the church in the first place, with certain reservations. A compromise was reached when part of the land was deeded back to the church and part to the library association. The Association then borrowed $2,000 and erected a beautiful little brick building which was the first permanent library structure in the town. The little library served the people from this building until George Willis Pack became the generous benefactor of the library.

It was also in 1879 that Christian Reid's book about the area, entitled *Land of the Sky*, was published and gave boosters a fitting phrase that would be applied to the Western North Carolina area to the present day.

At the beginning of the 1880's Asheville entered upon a tremendous brick building era. Many of the sturdy older structures still remaining as a basic foundation for the present modern metropolis were completed during this decade. It was a time of prosperity, a time of brisk travel, a time when a great many monied men were coming into the region.

The mountains were already drawing summer residents out of the hot, low lands of South Carolina and from the Piedmont plantations of North Carolina. These families came into the cool foothills carrying their

Baird Bottoms looked like this when the local train service ran from Asheville to Weaverville. This was to be the site of Beaver Lake and the surrounding area became Lake View Park residential section. Photo courtesy Pack Memorial Library

The *Perly-Crockett Lumber Company passenger train to the top of Mount Mitchell. This was a popular resort ride. Later a pleasure road was built along the old grade. Photo courtesy Pack Memorial Library*

way of life with them, all the household complete with servants and piles of luggage. They stayed all the summer months in houses built to resemble the mansions left behind.

At first, they ventured no further than the tentative rising foothills in upper South Carolina, hesitating to cross over the Blue Ridge to construct their large summer homes. What was clearly needed was easy transportation, a way in and out. The wealthy and powerful men had the answer to the problem.

Prior to the Civil War the Western North Carolina Railway had reached the lower ramparts of the Blue Ridge. From the east it came across the state to Morganton.

The Charlestonians of South Carolina were seeking a way over the steep wall of Saluda Mountain. As construction of the Western North Carolina Railway slowly snaked its way west from O. Henry Station near Old Fort, the engineers, home fresh from the war, employed a technique of throwing long curving loops of tracks up and around the sides of the mountains. Where this was impossible they bored tunnels through the mountains with "black powder" and hauled the dirt out with wheel barrows. Slowly, they climbed ever higher until the tracks reached Swannanoa. By 1882 they had "made it" up and over the ridge.

But Saluda was even more difficult. The builders were in a hurry. They were also bold and daring. They cut the trees and laid down rails length by length up and over the most rugged heights of Saluda and in so doing created at 4.7 percent, the steepest, standard gauge, regularly scheduled, main line east of the Rockies.

It was done. As the powerful black engines, burning coal and pouring smoke, came into and out of the Southern Highlands on their daily runs, they brought goods of every kind. They also brought people, lots of people, seeking out what the region had to give.

Asheville, the small back-country village, more recently shut-in by mountains, now was drawing the rich and stylish to its door. They came from everywhere.

Watching as the railroads approached from two directions, the citizens would have never believed that in so short a time, their village would become a prosperous and famous city, one where great and prestigious visitors would find a life as elegant and as luxurious as that to be enjoyed in almost any resort area in the county.

They also couldn't know and wouldn't realize that these visitors would drastically alter the character of their town. Widespread changes would begin immediately.

For one thing, with the incoming flux of people, Asheville had to begin thinking about paving the downtown streets. Before this, wooden boards kept down the dust in summer, the mud in winter. The first program was started in 1890, with the initial project being the paving of a section of South Main Street, beginning at Pack Square. A paved road was then often only hard packed layers of gravel, but this served far better than a mud-filled alleyway.

Charles D. Blanton, mayor of Asheville from 1889 through 1893, did a lot to project the town as a coming tourist and visitor center. It was during his term of office that the first streets were paved.

The public square, having been paved in 1890, became a center of business. Before this, the sidewalks had been only board planks laid end to end, and the Square mostly open mud holes where hogs wallowed about to the distress of the new visitors in town with their long dresses and finely tailored suits.

The method of paving by brick was adopted during Blanton's term of office, with the contractor being General P.M.B. Young. The bricks were laid meticulously, one by one, end to end and by hand, of course.

The street paving went a long way in making newcomers happier with the town and gradually the street paving program spread out down to the depot and off in other well traveled directions. Stones were laid down for sidewalks and later these became concrete.

One of the men who had become interested in Asheville was Col. Franklin Coxe. The Coxe family of Philadelphia was founded in North Carolina in Rutherford County by Franklin's father, Francis Sidney Coxe, and was one of wealth, tracing their lineage to the late 17th century in England and the court of King Charles II.

Franklin Coxe had coal interests in Pennsylvania. After the Civil War he had returned to North Carolina to become president of the Commercial National Bank in Charlotte. He moved back to Pennsylvania temporarily, but during his time in the South, Franklin Coxe had invested extensively in Asheville. With Col. A.C. Andrews he had helped construct the Western North Carolina Railroad and served as its vice president. But perhaps he is best known for his building of the first Battery Park Hotel.

Old Stony Hill to the north of the village was the highest nearby rise. Renamed Battery Porter after the war, it was here that Coxe chose to build his luxurious Queen Anne style hotel called the Battery Park

This Shay helped harvest the rich timberland in the Western North Carolina mountains. Thousands of acres in the southern mountains were denuded before a program of conservation was begun. Photo courtesy United States Forest Service

The coming of the railroads brought Asheville's first Golden Age and boom period. This picture was taken at Connelly Springs, North Carolina in 1891. Photo courtesy United States Forest Service

The first Battery Park Hotel was one of the largest and finest in the south. It was from the porch of this hotel that George Vanderbilt looked out toward Mt. Pisgah and decided to build his home here. Photo courtesy The Ball Collection, Southern Highlands Research Center, Asheville

Hotel. The rambling structure and the grounds covered 25 acres on top of the hill. It was 475 feet long, with many wings and wide verandas. The Battery Park opened in 1886, was one of the first class, fine hotels of the South and offered modern bathrooms, elevators, hot and cold water, dining rooms, a bowling alley and billiard rooms. Its ballroom became the social center of the town.

Coxe had other developments in Asheville, among them a row of commercial buildings along Government Street, now College Street.

Many distinguished visitors began coming to the Battery Park. The Eagle Hotel continued with a good business and there were other good hotels by this time. The Grand Central Hotel had been erected at Patton and Lexington Avenues. The Swannanoa was opened on the west side of South Main in 1880. It is thought the Swannanoa was the first Asheville hotel to contain a bathroom.

George Washington Vanderbilt began coming to Asheville in 1887, lured by the accommodations of the Battery Park and enchanted by the magnificent view of Pisgah Mountain and the rural farms to the south and west of the town.

Vanderbilt was the youngest son of William H. Vanderbilt and grandson of the "Commodore," Cornelius Vanderbilt, the wealthy shipping magnate of New York.

Vanderbilt had inherited great wealth. The story is told that he searched over the world for the most beautiful spot to build his home and after seeing the view, decided on Asheville. At any rate, he began quietly buying up land until he owned over 125,000 acres including Mt. Pisgah.

As the Vanderbilt agents began to contact the farmers and lay options upon their land, rumors began to circulate among the citizens. At first the purpose of the purchases was unknown, but it is a sure thing that as it became common knowledge that Vanderbilt would build his home at Asheville, no imagination could possibly picture the grand and elaborate edifice Biltmore House would eventually become.

A rarely seen picture, Biltmore Village as it is being built in 1895. All Souls Episcopal Church is to the left. The two story building in the center is the Estate office, still in use. The Biltmore Train Station may be seen two buildings to the right of this. The row of houses in the foreground were all to be torn down. The village was designed by R.S. Smith, the supervising architect of Biltmore House. Photo courtesy The Biltmore House and Gardens Archives

It is said that after searching the world over for "the most beautiful place," George W. Vanderbilt chose the Asheville area in which to build the most luxurious private residence in America. Photo courtesy Biltmore House and Gardens

Mrs. George W. Vanderbilt was beloved by the mountain women. She encouraged them to produce their handicrafts which were indigenous to the region and helped them to market their products. Photo courtesy Biltmore House and Gardens

Biltmore House under construction in the late 1880's. Photo courtesy Biltmore House and Garden Archives

The little town of Best south of Asheville was included in the purchases in its entirety. In fact, Best was to be completely leveled and a model English countryside village was constructed in its place.

Architects and artisans from the world over were brought in. From New York, Richard Morris Hunt, the architect who had designed the Fifth Avenue mansions of the Vanderbilts, came. The story is told of how Vanderbilt had first envisioned a much more modest white columned Southern plantation house on his land, but Richard Hunt soon convinced him it must be in the manner of a French chateau. It was a superb coming together of minds. Vanderbilt had traveled the world, spoke eight languages fluently, had a vast knowledge of art and fine furnishings, and had collected a library numbering in the thousands of volumes. The mansion was designed and constructed in exquisite taste. It most closely follows the style of the Francis I wing at Blois located in the Loire Valley of France.

Frederick Law Olmsted, who had designed Central Park in New York, was brought in to transform the farm land into magnificent gardens, forests and pasturelands for the pure bred Jersey cattle Vanderbilt planned to have on the estate.

Two architects who were to make a decided imprint on Asheville came to work for Vanderbilt. They were already mentioned, Rafael Guastavino and Richard Sharpe Smith. Guastavino settled in Black Mountain; Smith remained in Asheville to design a large number of residences and commercial buildings.

A railroad track was laid from a point near the present Biltmore Railway Station to the site of the house. All manner of construction materials were brought in daily.

The foundations began to take shape on a superbly located rise upon which a single pine tree had

Biltmore House from the lagoon. Photo by Lou Harshaw

stood out against the sky, attracting Vanderbilt's attention. The entire six floor footage of the house was to total four acres. The house was to contain more than 200 rooms with a facade of 780 feet.

As the main structure began to rise at its various levels, its towers and vertical Gothic elements were enhanced by tall narrow windows and steeply pitched roofs. Every corner was detailed by gargoyles, pinnacles, and chimneys.

Vanderbilt began to organize his estate into a "productive enterprise," creating a farm department, a forestry and a landscape department, all being headed by the most knowledgeable people available to him in each of these fields. It was to be a working farm with a variety of interests.

A lot of the estate acreage was in forests, but a lot was also in small farms. It remained for Olmsted to transform all this into intricate formal gardens, wildflower gardens and sweeping pastures for the cattle. Fountains, pools and a large lake came into being under the capable hands of the workers.

Construction had begun in 1889 and a little over five years later the house was officially opened on Christmas Eve, 1895, with a family party described in both the Asheville newspapers and *The New York Times.* Vanderbilt was unmarried and 26 years old when he began the Western North Carolina estate project. The house had been completed for three years when Vanderbilt married Edith Stuyvesant Dresser, a direct descendant of Peter Stuyvesant, and the couple had one child, a daughter named Cornelia.

The name Biltmore is derived from Bildt, the Dutch town from which the family's forebears came (van der Bildt), and "moor," an old English word for rolling upland country.

Hunt and Vanderbilt worked together on the interior, bringing together designs and styles of four centuries, including Louis XV, Louis VVI, Jacobean, Francis I and many others.

Susanne Brendel-Pandich, Curator of Biltmore House, in an article for *Antiques* magazine of April 1980, writes of an entry Mrs. Hunt made in her diary detailing a visit they made in 1889, "to the oriental carpet warehouse of Robinson in London, where Vanderbilt bought three hundred rugs for the still unbuilt house, and then went on to Brussels to look for tapestries."

Again, Brendel-Pandich says in her article: "Many details remained unfinished, but by the late 1890's

The conservatory and greenhouse at Biltmore House were completely rebuilt on the original lines in 1957. They face the Walled Garden which covers four acres. The lower section contains the Rose Garden with about 5,000 plants. Photo by Dick and Lou Harshaw

Detail stone carvings on the outside of the spiral grand staircase at Biltmore House. Photo Dick Harshaw

George Vanderbilt's ideals were realized. In addition to the house, landscaped roads, and a five hundred acre landscaped park, the estate included a dairy, truck farm, chicken farm, pig farm, nurseries and tenant farmhouses. These and other farming projects were headed by the farm manager, G.E. Weston."

Auxiliary buildings on the estate were in the style of English manor houses, with pebble dash-stucco walls, brick quoins, and pantile roofs.

The little village of Best was renamed Biltmore Village and with the picturesque All Souls Church as the focal point, included a number of residences, stores, a railroad station, school, hospital, post office and a recreation hall. For the most part, Biltmore Village was created to house those employed in estate related positions.

The untimely death of Vanderbilt after an appendectomy, in 1914, blunted the future development of Biltmore for a time as an income producing, many-faceted enterprise. In 1920, his widow sold some 90,000 acres of forest lands at a very low price to the Department of the Interior, and this acreage became the nucleus of Pisgah National Forest.

Cornelia Vanderbilt had married John Francis Amherst Cecil of England, whose lineage dated back to William Cecil, Lord Burghley, Secretary to Queen Elizabeth I. After years of excellent service to the Queen, Cecil died in 1598, at which time the Queen chose his son, Robert Cecil, Earl of Salisbury, to take his place.

Biltmore House like any great lady studies herself in her "mirror," the reflecting pool in front of the house. Photo by Dick Harshaw

Detail work of stone carving at Biltmore House. Photo by Lou Harshaw

The fine wines bottled under the Biltmore label is a new industry for the Biltmore House and Gardens. Photo courtesy Biltmore House and Gardens Archives by Michael Kent Smith

The newly cultivated vineyards at Biltmore House. This is the first commerical wine making industry in the southeast. Photo courtesy Biltmore House and Gardens Archives by Michael Kent Smith

After the death of Queen Elizabeth, it was Cecil who quietly made the arrangements for crowning James VI of Scotland, who then became James I of England, uniting the two countries.

The Cecils made Biltmore their home, and from this marriage two sons were born, George H.V., and William A.V., the present owners of the estate.

The affairs of Biltmore in the years following the death of Vanderbilt were carried on by two dedicated and brilliant men: Chauncey Delos Beadle, who was first hired as assistant to Olmsted, remained on the estate until his death in 1950 at age 85 as superintendent, and Judge Junius G. Adams of Asheville, whom Mrs. Vanderbilt employed to serve as overall counsellor.

As William Cecil says in his book, *Biltmore*, "The Jersey herd was amongst the finest in the United States and Biltmore Dairy Farms under E.D. Mitchel was becoming an outstanding regional dairy."

George Cecil studied under Mitchell and became president of Biltmore Dairy Farms, Inc.

The Asheville Chamber of Commerce persuaded the estate interests in 1930 to open the house and grounds to the public.

Since that time many changes have swept over the house and grounds. The huge house remains the same structure, though Olmsted's gardens and parks have grown full and lush, the most outstanding estate gardens in the South.

The interior of the house has gone through two major and a number of minor, renovations. Over the years, additional portions of the house have been opened to the public. Last year, the downstairs or service rooms of the house were opened for a separate public tour section.

A portion of the estate was developed into the Town of Biltmore Forest, a residential section of large and lavish homes.

On the estate grounds new interests have created two new major projects. Over a million dollars was spent in recent years in renovating a huge barn into a modern restaurant, Deerpark. It is rapidly becoming known for its distinctive cuisine fashioned after the elaborate picnics held on the estate by the Vanderbilts.

After a great deal of study, a new wine industry has been started with the development of vineyards on the grounds. The wines are bottled under the Biltmore label. This is a "first" for a commercial wine industry in this part of the country, but seemingly the lands of the estate have proven ideal for further future development in the market.

Modern road building interrupted the peace and quiet of the estate when the Blue Ridge Parkway was constructed along its southern border. More massive road projects took place when Interstate Route 40 was built along another section of the southern border and opened on April 15, 1967. Interstate Route 26 came in from east to west across the central portion of the estate and opened on July 31, 1968.

According to Walter Cochran of the Department of Transportation, every effort was made for cooperation between estate interests and the road builders to preserve as much as possible the tranquillity of the grounds of the estate and yet construct efficient serviceable highways to carry the growing number of vehicles over the throughways.

Extensive planning by the road builders and estate officials resulted in maintaining the surrounding countryside vistas. From the gentle curving of Olmsted's roads the rock-faced surfaces of the interstate bridges do not shock the senses.

The many benefits down through the years of the Vanderbilt interests to the Asheville community are almost incalculable.

Mrs. George Vanderbilt took a great interest in the mountain people, especially the women, who had a tradition of fine handiwork but no markets. She established Biltmore Industries in 1901 as a craft guild which to this day produces fine handloomed woolen materials.

Among the crafts taught and perpetuated were carving, furniture making, stamp boxes, book ends, toys and other objects. Also made were woven baskets and quilts. It was the interest of Mrs. Vanderbilt, which helped revive and expand handicraft in the southern mountains, enabling them in later years to have a sizeable impact on local economy.

Some of the most extensive benefits to come to us from the Biltmore interests revolve around two men who deserve a chapter all their own, but perhaps we will confine ourselves to the more important details of the story, and reserve their full and complete history for another time.

These were two men of the forests. Vanderbilt employed Gifford Pinchot, the first trained forester in this country and later Governor of Pennsylvania, to plan and direct the renovations of the woodlands. As the Biltmore House and Gardens visitor guidebook puts it: "The result was the first comprehensive forest

The new Deerpark Restaurant on Biltmore Estate. More than a million dollars was spent in renovation and new construction of the restaurant. Photo courtesy Biltmore House and Gardens Archives by Michael Kent Smith

plan in the Western Hemisphere. Supervision was needed to the extensive planting, the establishing of experimental areas and the lumbering of the large tracts west of the French Broad River. Dr. Carl A. Schenck (1868-1955) of Darmstadt, Germany, was brought over to be chief Forester.''

Dr. Schenck, with Vanderbilt's approval and sponsorship, founded the Biltmore School of Foresty in 1898, the first forestry school in America.

Pinchot, after his work at Biltmore, went on to become head of the newly created agency that was to become the National Forest Service. He was nationally and internationally known for his innovative forest practices.

Dr. Schenck taught many of the foresters who later were to dominate the field in this country for many years.

The school, contained in several log and wood buildings just off the Blue Ridge Parkway on Highway

The Italian Gardens at Biltmore House contain three formal pools. Photo by Lou Harshaw

276 South, to the west of Asheville, has been restored by the National Forest Service and is open to the public. For many years the tiny school has been called "The Cradle of Forestry in America."

Together, Pinchot and Schenck are responsible for many of the methods used in the preservation and maintenance of the valuable timberlands left in America today.

William Cecil is president of the Biltmore Company and as he said in his book, "If vision is given to any of us, and if any of us have the wisdom to use it, the 'lady on the hill' (Biltmore House) shows that survival in our day and age is not only possible but certain. Not in any retrogressive sense, but with confidence that all need not be temporary and mundane; that preservation of the good of our ancestors for the benefit of our descendants is truly the American reality."

Friends of the author, Sallie and Charles Thomason endeavor to make friends with one of the Biltmore House lions at the main entrance to the house. Photo by Lou Harshaw

Richard Morris Hunt was the world famous architect who designed Biltmore House at Asheville. Hunt had designed the Fifth Avenue mansions of the Vanderbilts, but it remained for the Biltmore House at Asheville to be the crowning masterpiece of his life's work. Photo courtesy Biltmore House and Gardens

Frederick Law Olmsted designed Central Park in New York City. He was employed by George W. Vanderbilt to transform some 100,000 Western North Carolina acres of small farms and woodlands into the magnificent Biltmore Gardens of today. Photo courtesy Biltmore House and Gardens

CHAPTER V

The Greatest Benefactor

IN his article on George Willis Pack, written for the 90th Anniversary edition of *The Asheville Citizen-Times*, Doug Reed who was at the time a staff writer for the paper says:

"He was the greatest benefactor Asheville ever had.

"That was the confident judgment of his own generation. Time has not altered it.

"In the sands of local history, the footprints of George Willis Pack are those of a great man. They may be obscured, but they cannot be erased."

Pack came to Asheville from the north in the spring of 1884. Physicians had advised him to bring his wife south to the city for her health. They stopped at the Swannanoa Hotel.

It was evident that Pack was taken by the city. That spring he began to construct a large home on what is now Merrimon Avenue.

Pack was a rich man. He had made his large fortune from his part of a small lumber company, and from his judicious businesss management his assets grew and expanded into a number of large forestry operations.

Leaving his obligations in the north to be carried on by younger associates, Pack soon moved into his new home, which he called "Manyoaks."

Now, the legendary benefactor has almost been forgotten. Few of the tide of summer visitors and not many of the permanent citizens know the story that lies behind the name of Pack for which the most important and central open "square" of Asheville is named.

For all his wealth, for all his business acumen, George Pack was never a seeker of glory, never desired great public acclaim. He wished only to fulfill his duties as a private citizen to a town he obviously loved.

It was soon known that Pack was quietly providing funds for a number of widow and orphans, both of the white and black races. His first benefaction for the general public was made on June 4, 1892, when he provided funds for the Sarah Garrison Kindergarten for the Asheville Free Kindergarten Association.

He purchased a lot for $600 in North Asheville on the east side of East Street between Seney and Hillside. (Seney Street has since disappeared.)

Pack employed the architectural firm of Wills Brothers to design the school house. Mrs. O.M. Quayle, superintendent of the school, was to supervise the arrangement of the rooms. On a bid of $1,650, Milton Hardin was chosen to build it, exclusive of painting. The total cost, including grading and fencing, ran around $3,000. Pack then donated the school as a gift to the association.

Pack was to continue to assist the school. He paid the salary of one of its teachers for the rest of his life and provided annually for about one fourth of the cost of operating the school.

At left, view of the area to be landscaped into Pack Square and the City-County Plaza. The Jackson Building for years, was the tallest building in the city. The flag draped building on the right is the new fire station and police station. Photo courtesy The Ball Collection, Southern Highlands Research Center, Asheville

Pack Square (below) was a busy thoroughfare for all kinds of traffic during the late 1890's. The street cars are running, the new automobiles are becoming plentiful and there are still some horses and buggies to be seen. People also seem to be enjoying strolling on foot around the Square. The Vance Monument has replaced the old Crystal Fountain and a new fountain has been built on the site where the Courthouse stood. The spire of Central Methodist Church may be seen in the upper left of the picture. The post office tower is just left of the Vance Monument and the old Battery Park Hotel is still queen of the city. Photo courtesy The Ball Collection, Southern Highlands Research Center, Asheville

71

The crowd is waiting for the "boys" to return from the First World War. The little concrete building in the lower right hand corner is an information booth for visitors. It is thought that the little wagon in front of it was to use to take photographs of visitors. The building at the right with the tower is the first George Willis Pack Memorial Library. The Jackson Building has not gone up at this time. Photo courtesy The Ball Collection, Southern Highlands Research Center, Asheville

George Willis Pack, a man of great wealth and distinction, loved his adopted town of Asheville and did more for the city than anyone else in its history by his donations of lands and monies for its cultural progress. Photo courtesy Pack Memorial Library

The kindergarten was established to provide less fortunate children with a foundation for further education. It was later to be incorporated into Asheville's public school system.

According to the Reed article: "The public square at that time was dominated by a big three story courthouse, with a bell tower, that stood at the east end. On the south side of the square were the First National Bank and Daily Citizens buildings."

Pack felt the square should be cleared of the courthouse and be beautified and preserved for all time as an open public place. He felt a new courthouse should be erected in some other section of the city.

In conversations with George S. Powell, Pack learned of the desire of some of the town's prominent citizens to erect a monument to the memory of Sen. Z.B. Vance, North Carolina's Civil War governor, born in Buncombe County. He had died two years before.

It was hoped, Powell explained to Pack, that the square might be used for the monument. Pack agreed that Vance must, if possible, be honored.

Without prior notice, the county commissioners received the following unpretentious letter, written by Pack on May 30, 1896:

"Gentlemen: If the County of Buncombe will give the land in front of the courthouse for a site for a monument in honor of Zebulon B. Vance, I will give $2,000 toward the erection of such a monument. Your obedient servant, Geo. W. Pack."

In his wise way, Pack had contributed enough to ensure the building of the monument, but he had left a challenge for the delighted commissioners and townsfolk to raise the rest of the funds.

One thousand, three hundred dollars was raised over the next year, with an initial gift of $100 to get the fund going by *The Asheville Citizen.*

On ground breaking day, John Z. Jordan turned the first shovel of dirt. The cornerstone was laid December 22, 1897, with full Masonic rites and lengthy oratory. It was to be completed about five months later.

Pack had no public part in any of this, preferring to remain in the background. He may have been on one of his many trips abroad at that time, but at any rate it was never his way to seek the limelight.

In 1898, Pack donated the Swannanoa Club grounds and golf links to members of that organization.

From the Doug Reed article we learn that Pack contributed large sums of money for relief during the severe winter of 1898 and 1899. Upon learning during the Spanish American War that the Asheville boys in the First North Carolina Regiment needed money to tide them over to the government payday, he sent them $500. Later, when the young soldiers insisted on repaying the entire amount, it is said Pack was so moved that he wept.

Pack's generous gifts to the city were always without fanfare. Sometimes the recipients were not aware that this kind-hearted and generous man even knew of their needs. Thus, when Haywood Parker, president of the Asheville Library Association, received the following letter, he was almost overcome.

"Dear Sirs: I offer to puchase from its present owner, the Palmetto Building, formerly the First National Bank Building, with the land appertaining thereto and give it to the Asheville Library, with the understanding that the Library shall be installed in the large room formerly occupied by the bank, and that the corporation shall be free from debt when it receives the conveyance of the property.

"I will remove the bank vault and do the necessary work to prepare for the library, but will not supply

The new Buncombe County Courthouse under construction on land donated to the city by George Willis Pack. It is one of the largest county buildings in the state. A corner of the old Courthouse can be seen in the lower right hand side of the picture. Photo courtesy The Ball Collection, Southern Highlands Research Center, Asheville

furniture or lighting fixtures. The property to be conveyed and possession given on or before April 1, 1899. Yours respectfully, Geo. W. Pack."

Pack was again following the pattern of offering enough to make certain the project could be accomplished, but also leaving enough undone to make sure the local citizens would have a great part of the work to do and could be proud of their own accomplishments.

During the year 1896, the need for a new courthouse was discussed by the County Commissioners. When they decided to advertise for a site, either to be purchased or traded for the site on the square, it evoked in the newspaper suggestions from many citizens suggesting sites ranging from Church Street to the "Pack property on College Street."

This hint, if it was such. made by Locke Craig, a prominent young lawyer who later served as governor of the state, went unmatched by Pack at that time.

At any rate, the County Commissioners faced other financial problems in an expanding community as the year 1900 drew to a close. They met on January 1, in a mass gathering of officials and taxpayers to discuss their growing success.

The large group was totally unprepared when W.B. Gwyn took the floor.

He then read the astonished people the following letter: "To the Commissioners of the county of Buncombe: I offer to give to the county, to be used for a site for a courthouse and county offices, the land on College street in Asheville which I purchased from Col. A.T. Davidson, provided that the county will dedicate to the public, forever, to be used for the purposes of a public square or place, whatever land the county may now own within the limits of the public square, so called, in Asheville, the present courthouse to be removed therefrom prior to such date as you may agree upon with Judge Merriman and Mr. Gwyn, acting for me, December 31, 1900, George W. Pack."

Pack's property, which he was offering to the county, lay on the southside of College and joining the Knickerbocker boarding house property on the west. An old mansion stood on it in a grove of huge trees. The lot had a frontage of 210 feet and a depth of more than 400. the property was a great financial value.

Pack in his traditional way left challenges. Funds of somewhere between $50,000 to $100,000 would have to be raised to build the courthouse.

The county, in a later transaction, deeded the property on the square to the city at which time it was named Pack Square.

The Buncombe County Courthouse has been torn down on Pack Square and a new fountain has just been built on the the site where it stood. This photograph (left) shows in detail the City Hall now the eastern "wall" of the Square. This building also contained the fire department and the Asheville city market where farmers brought their produce for sale every day. Photo courtesy The Ball Collection, Southern Highlands Research Center, Asheville

After the Courthouse that stood on Pack Square was torn down this graceful building (right) was erected on land donated by George Willis Pack. This Courthouse was opened in 1903. It was used only a few years. The "boom" period of the 1920's left it outdated and too small. Photo courtesy The Ball Collection, Southern Highlands Research Center, Asheville

This unusual view shows the Sulphur Springs Hotel in West Asheville built by Edwin George Carrier. Carrier was the main developer of the large area west of the city lying across the French Broad River. Photo courtesy Pack Memorial Library

These were not the extent of the gifts of George Willis Pack to the city. In 1900 he had deeded property at the corner of Flint and Magnolia Streets as a park.

Montford Avenue Park was donated by Pack. In 1902 and 1903 he donated $1,000 to the YMCA, then struggling for funds to construct a building. He gave the city 13 acres for a park, now known as Aston Park. He gave $5,000 to the old Mission Hospital, and gave it another $5,000 at a later date. In 1905 and 1906 Pack gave sums to other hospitals. The exact amounts are now unknown.

In 1903 public funds had been subscribed in the amount of $150 so that a portrait of Pack could be painted.

It was hung in the courthouse between the portrait of Zebulon B. Vance and General R.B. Vance. In the ceremonial remarks made by Locke Craig on the date of the hanging, January 19, 1904, he said: "He made these gifts not at the request of anyone, needed though they were, indispensable as they now appear, they always came to us as a surprise. They were all the result of his own generous impulse: They were made not as an invtiation for praise or flattery, but modestly, unostentatiously, with no self laudation—he gave because he wanted to give."

Pack could not hear these remarks. His health was failing and he remained at his Southampton home on Long Island. He was never to return to his beloved mountain town.

On August 31, 1906, at the age of 75, Pack died.

Pack Square has survived several metamorphoses since George Willis Pack dreamed of how it should look and generously gave of his wealth to make it so. Even today, the Square is being rebuilt into a stylish new form with modern structures rising. The old courthouse Pack helped bring into being long ago outlived its usefulness and a still newer one arose on another part of the land he gave.

But the memorial to another man remains, the Zebulon B. Vance memorial for which Pack was mostly responsible. So maybe the tall spire can help us remember two great men. The tall spire and the name Pack Square which, along with Pack Memorial Library, are our reminder of a wise and generous citizen.

Another man who meant a great deal in the growth and progress of the city in the latter 1880's was Edwin George Carrier.

In 1885, he and his family were on a trip from their home in Pennsylvania to Florida when they passed through Asheville. Immediately impressed by its beauty, climate and friendly atmosphere, they decided to settle in the little town.

Carrier had already garnered a fortune in the lumber business of the north, so there were ample funds to carry out his plans. Shortly after his arrival, he purchased the first several hundred of what would become 1,200 acres of land west and north of the French Broad River, including the Sulphur Springs and J.P. Gaston properties. He formed the West Asheville Improvement Company and began the modern development of West Asheville.

Carrier, as the first of his projects, built in 1886 the Sulphur Springs Hotel over the site of the Colonel Deaver's old wooden hotel, which had been destroyed by fire in 1862 during the Civil War. The new hotel, a three-story brick structure, became one of Western North Carolina's most popular tourist resorts.

Its name changed first to Carrier's Springs and then to The Belmont. In 1889, a wing was added that contained the first passenger elevator in the South.

In 1889, Carrier built a low wooden dam across Hominy Creek and constructed a power house plant. It was a small wooden building equipped with a 60 horsepower turbine and a 40 kilowatt generator. The power plant was distinguished for two reasons: it was the first hydroelectric plant in Western North Carolina; and also the first of its kind to furnish power for a commercial street car. It provided the first reliable electric lights in Asheville after its service to The Belmont.

That same year Carrier built a high 250 foot steel bridge which was the engineering feat of the day. The bridge spanned the French Broad River at the junction with the Swannanoa and was known as Carrier's Bridge.

The hotel, leased by Dr. Carl Von Ruck in October, 1891, for ten years, burned to the ground on August 24, 1892. Over the next several days the charred ruins drew thousands to the spot.

Construction began in 1890 on the West Asheville and Sulphur Springs Electric Railway to the Springs.

The line ran from the vicinity of the Southern passenger station across Carrier's Bridge along the present Amboy Road and up by Hominy Creek to Sulphur Springs and The Belmont.

Granted a franchise by Asheville Board of Aldermen in October, 1891, Carrier extended his line on into the city. It went along Depot Street, Bartlett Street and French Broad Avenue to the corner of West College and North Main Street, ending at Government Street and what is now Haywood Street and Battery Park Place.

Plans for any further extension were strongly opposed by the Asheville Street Railway Company, which had secured in 1888 the "Farinholt franchise" and opened in 1889, with Dr. S. Westry Battle, E.D. Davidson and Colonel James G. Martin as its developers. They did not want Carrier to cross their line.

Carrier, being a man of ingenious methods, gathered a few trusted men of his company together and on a dark night laid the track and completed the crossing. The Carrier men then hand pushed a car across the new track, thus dismissing any possibility of an injunction.

Carrier was the area's first developer of modern day dairying, cattle raising and orchard work. He was the first to bring in pure bred Herefords and Jersey cattle to his West Asheville land.

He was one of the first sponsors of the Western North Carolina good roads program.

Among his other projects was the completion of a race track in early 1892 along the French Broad River bottom for the entertainment of his Hotel Belmont Guests. Training and racing horses were favorite hobbies. The large tract of land also served as a Fair Grounds and was used for baseball games, bicycle

Asheville is changing. The Majestic Theatre, one of Asheville's first movie houses is open. **The Asheville Times,** *not yet merged with the* **Citizen,** *is at home in the center of the block on College Street. Spruce Street goes down to the side where the "Printing" sign of The Inland Press may be seen. Note the brick paved streets. The church building in the background is that of the First Baptist Church. It was built in the 1889's and was torn down when the Baptists moved to the present building at Oak and Woodfin Streets in 1927. Photo courtesy The Ball Collection, Southern Highlands Research Center, Asheville*

races, trotting races, tournaments of the Field of Gold and many other community activities. It soon became known as Carrier's Field.

Daily crowds of more than 1,500 came to enjoy the varied activities that took place at the region's first large and popular sports field.

The twin tragedies of the loss of Carrier's hotel and his orange groves in Florida drew Carrier away from Asheville back to his first financial interest, the lumber business. Even though he spent the latter 20 years of his life away from the city, his body was returned after his death in March, 1927, and was buried in Riverside Cemetery.

Carrier was the man most responsible for the development of the large area west of the French Broad. He gave it the first easy access. He built the first large luxurious hotel and gave immeasurable pleasure and relaxation through his sports sponsorships.

Carrier—the name still lingers as an echo in the mind for those of this generation who grew up in Asheville, if not as a reality on a place or structure, it is a reminder of a true pioneer, of his life and times.

The decade of the 1880's had wrought a tremendous change in Asheville. In the space of a ten year period the small, rural village had become a growing, thriving town. The coming of the railroads had been mostly responsible. The snaking of those gleaming steel rails carrying the huge black engines and their endless lines of freight cars and Pullmans brought hundreds of people into the remote areas of the Southern Appalachians. True, sometimes even the most powerful of the massive steam locomotives still labored mightily up the steep grades. But the train was the most comfortable and fastest method of travel man had experienced, and he was lured on the road in great numbers. In addition to passengers, all manner of goods could be transported to the mountain area.

Some of the significant events of this period have already been detailed. There are others that should be mentioned.

The Board of Trade, later to become the Asheville Chamber of Commerce, was organized in 1882. That same year a hook and ladder company was established to fight fires.

Asheville installed public waterworks in 1884, and Memorial Mission Hospital opened.

The streetcar system was built in 1888, and the town's first public schools opened. Electric streetlights were on for the first time in that year, and the town installed the first telephones and a sewer system.

The next year a railway was built up Sunset Mountain and became a favorite pleasure ride for the young courting crowd.

That same year, the YMCA was organized.

In 1890, another newspaper, *The Asheville Advertiser*, was founded. Some of the earlier newspapers had long gone out of business, of course. Kenilworth Inn was opened in 1890, and free mail delivery went into effect.

We are indebted to the 90th Anniversary Edition of *The Asheville Citizen Times* for the above dates and for informing us that Asheville's first city hall and marketplace was built in 1892. The site was on the east side of Pack Square. The post office building went up at the corner of Patton Avenue and Haywood Street, on the triangle that is now Pritchard Park.

The first automobile arrived in Asheville in 1898, a Locomobile Steamer sent in by the Octagon Soap Company. The car was delivered to a grocery store owned by Clarence Sawyer, who then drove it up and down Asheville streets. The first automobile to be owned by an Ashevillian was a two-cylinder Brennen built in 1900 by Eugene Sawyer, brother of Clarence. A year later he purchased a single seater Locomobile Steamer that provided the city with its first real car.

J.P. Coston and Ernest Alexander bought a two-cylinder Locomobile steam surrey. J.E. Rumbough purchased a Centaur Electric.

Paying $950 in 1902, Tench Coxe became the owner of a single cylinder Cadillac and the following year, for $2,750, he purchased a White Steamer.

Dr. James Sawyer purchased a one-cylinder Cadillac in 1903. A one-cylinder Cadillac passenger touring car was bought by Frank Coxe.

With the coming of the first Ford in 1905, the spurt of automobile buying speeded up, and by the next year there were about 35 cars in the city.

Clarence Sawyer bought the first delivery truck in 1906, a one-cylinder Cadillac which was driven about the streets for more than 15 years by Alonzo McCoy, a Black man.

E.W. Grove brought into Asheville what was probably the largest machine in the early days of the automobile. It was a finely-made four cylinder, 30 to 50 horsepower Pope-Toledo.

Dr. Grove and his chauffeur, H. McDonald, drove the car from Asheville to St. Louis and back, a remarkable trip for the times and the roads.

The first macadam road was built from Smith's Bridge into West Asheville in 1897.

The Square had acquired an old world look in the decade. According to Richard Thornton: "With the coming of brick structures in the 1880's, there was a strong Scottish-Northern European feeling. The building during the Victorian period was not decorative. The style was very practical, simple, typical of the small cities of Northern Europe. The buildings lacked decorative details. They were pragmatic in feeling, almost Germanic in style."

Thornton brings up the question of whether this feeling of the architecture was intentional or not. Did the influx of foreign artisans and architects consciously impose their views upon their buildings?

At any rate, as the end of the century approached, Asheville was a unique Mountain City. It had none of the flavor of typical Southern post Civil War towns.

A photograph of that time shows a large open square closed on four sides by interesting buildings housing a variety of commercial establishments, ranging from photographic studios to cafes, lawyers' and doctors' offices. There are many people in the photograph, and transportation varies from those on foot to horse drawn wagons, electric street cars and some few of the first models of automobiles.

It was late in the last decade of the century that Asheville was beginning on a new phase of development, another facet of its character would emerge, one that would spread word of the city over the entire nation and again cause a large migration into the region. The migration would include the rich and the poor. They would be drawn in, all for one cause in common—their health.

It was "Judge" Edward Aston, mayor of Asheville in 1880, who first started promoting the city as a health resort. "Judge" Aston had written letters and mailed out thousands of promotional brochures extolling the town's benefits for those suffering from tuberculosis or lung disease. His advertising drew many prominent physicians who remained to open hospitals and sanitariums. The circulars also attracted prominent people, suffering from some health problem, who remained to invest their money and open businesses.

Among the best known of the sanitariums was Winyah, started by Dr. Carl von Ruck. Soon Asheville's climate, clean air and pure water were among its assets in fighting "consumption," as it was sometimes called.

By 1890, the population had reached 10,000.

The growing prosperity of the town was not to last. The first, relatively easily made fortunes became for many "paper profits." Values rapidly became inflated. Speculations were made with non-existent cash, and eventually came the inevitable "crash." Banks failed, the real estate market went dead and a period of stagnation followed which withered the expansion of the town.

Bad as it was, the slump didn't last long and it didn't completely dampen the spirits of the investors and promoters of Asheville. While the Manor Hotel on Charlotte Street was the only major building project to go up at the end of the century, the beginning of the 1900's would see new money, new ideas and new personalities begin to exert influence over the mountain city. They would create an excitement, an energy that would build to fever pitch.

The barometer of business would go up and up, reaching a level never experienced before.

But in the hiatus that took place between the crash of the late 1890's and the frantic financial firestorm that would develop in the first quarter of the new century, life in the little town proceeded at a slow and leisurely pace.

Most of the large houses, set back from the quiet streets, were wrapped in long porches. In the evenings, at the end of the hot summer days, the porches were social gathering places. "Neighbors" strolling along tree lined avenues frequently stopped to chat, the young people clustered together on the steps, the older members in comfortable porch rockers. It was not unusual for three generations to exist in relative harmony in one residence. Since these consisted of many rooms it was easy to withdraw from any personal conflicts arising from close family living.

The gathering dusk brought out the "fire flies" and the katydids. Women wore their dresses to the ground. Men wore suits and ties, heavy wool in winter, but if a man so chose, he might change to white linen in summer.

There were no television sets, of course, few radios and few telephones. These were both status symbols of the times. An automobile was also a status symbol.

The newspapers carried the news, but there was also gossip. Carried with great relish by the "day" servants from one household to another, gathering in the process exaggeration and sometimes fabrication.

As they came into the town, the "fashionable" brought their own set of social rules. Ladies had to spend a great deal of time concerning themselves with just the proper dress for each occasion. There were clothes for tennis, clothes for golf, clothes for morning, clothes for afternoon. Untold hours were spent in ironing fine table linens each week, and woe be to the lady whose tablecloth displayed a wrinkle.

But for all this Asheville was never destined to be the typical Southern small town. Its sturdy middle income stock had come in two or three generations from land holding, independent minded, frontier families. There were few large plantations holding large numbers of black slaves. In the mountains, the owner worked the land right along side of his "help."

The peaceful atmosphere that existed at the end of the century was shortly to be shattered.

In the upcoming wild and ruinous land speculation that was to draw in almost every businessman in town and drastically change the lives of some, just about everybody in town would participate and thus be affected by the inevitable catastrophic events.

Lives, dreams and fortunes would be shattered in the space of a day's time. But before that happened, the little town experienced another golden age, an unbelievable fairy-tale time of good fortune made possible by high-rolling envisionists.

The Berkley Hotel (right) was located on the corner of Patton and Lexington Avenues where the present Kress building now stands. In 1905 the Swannanoa Hotel and the Berkley merged. Photo courtesy Pack Memorial Library

When the Berkley Hotel merged with the Swannanoa and moved, a locally owned department store, Bon Marche, established by Louis Lipinski, Sr. renovated the building and moved from a location on Biltmore Avenue (South Main Street). Photo courtesy The Ball Collection, Southern Highlands Research Center, Asheville

*The baroque Kenilworth Inn. It was to burn
in a terrible and costly fire. The manager lost
his life and though none of the guests were
killed, many lost thousands of dollars in
valuable jewelry and other possessions. Photo
courtesy Pack Memorial Library*

A haunting stillness settles over the ruins of Kenilworth Inn protographed on the morning after the fire, April 15, 1909. Photo courtesy Pack Memorial Library

ins og Kenilworth Inn.
Asheville N.C.

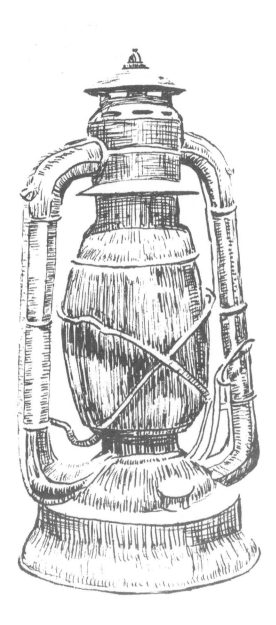

CHAPTER VI

Amazing Events and Prestigious People

THE second Golden Age of Asheville began to gain momentum right after the turn of the century. Each year during the first decade of the 1900's would bring amazing events and prestigious people to the growing mountain town. The population figure was now 14,694. In a relatively short period it would double that.

Time had given the little town a hundred turbulent years. In these years, the city had become more cosmopolitan, its citizenship more diverse than perhaps any other like-size metropolis of the South. Three distinct layers of culture had emerged. There was the bedrock foundation of native Scotch-Irish stock, many of whom were wealthy and politically influential. Another segment was composed of families of wealth and power who had vested their interests permanently within the region. The third element of the population was composed of the "floating" summer visitor set. This was a mixture that really never "mixed" socially very much.

As the century turned from old to new, one of the prominent men who were drawn to Asheville and who would leave his mark on its modern development was E.W. Grove of St. Louis.

He had come first in 1900, bringing his family for a visit. His doctor had recommended he seek out Asheville and the mountain climate in an effort to help cure a bronchial ailment.

Grove had amassed a great deal of money in the manufacture and sale of a patent medicine, Grove's Chill Tonic and Bromo Quinine.

During his visit he was greatly impressed with all he saw and began making plans to move to the city.

In 1905, Grove started buying up huge tracts of land on Sunset Mountain. He laid out an exclusive residential section which immediately began to draw members of the social crowd who built large mansion style homes. Their architecture is fascinating since most adhered in their planning to the hilly terrain, allowing in their design for the slopes and heavily forested areas.

But Grove dreamed on an even larger scale. Soon, acting as his own architect, he had builders hauling in massive boulders and removing a part of the mountainside to construct Grove Park Inn, which today remains as a great "wonder" of a building. Its overhanging red-tiled roofs still shelter visitors in the luxurious surroundings Grove envisioned.

Grove, in 1923, bought up the Battery Park Inn property and began to steam shovel away the rise on which the hotel stood. He moved the dirt to a deep ravine which ran along the side of Coxe Avenue, and thus transformed what was useless property into valuable business real estate.

He built, at the east end of the hill, a new Battery Park Hotel, tall (its seventh floor was level with the

In 1922, Asheville's most famous landmark was going. Even the mountain was being moved. The old Battery Park Hotel had seen great days of glory, long nights of bright lights and gaiety. Now, a new generation had new ideas. Photo courtesy The Ball Collection, Southern Highlands Research Center, Asheville

top of the Battery Park hill before its removal) and stately looking. The new brick hotel was more efficient, but much less elegant than the old.

When the land stretched level in front of the new hotel, Grove proceeded with his plans for an unusual structure which would house a number of shops and business offices.

According to the magazine *North Carolina Architect* of July/August, 1978, "This grand arcade covered a city block and was built of stone and terra cotta tile with Gothicized ornament inside and out. The building is a cross plan incorporating intersecting arcades. In the central section the interior space is

The dirt from Battery Park Hill as it was hauled away was used to fill a large ravine along the side of Coxe Avenue thus making the land usable for business purposes. Photo courtesy The Ball Collection, Southern Highlands Research Center, Asheville

open three stories to a skylight roof. Open balconies run on both sides on each floor and sweeping spiral staircases connect the first and second floors."

Unfortunately, Grove died before the office tower, with which the arcade was to be crowned, was completed.

Grove's son-in-law, Fred L. Seeley, who worked with him on his projects, chose one of the most spectacular sites near the city to construct his home.

Few motorists coming into the city over Tunnel Road from the east miss the massive landmark of

The shadow of the new Battery Park looms over a few remaining old houses in what has become Asheville's "downtown." The massiveness of the old auditorium building can be appreciated when it is compared to the George Vanderbilt Hotel beside it. Photo courtesy The Ball Collection, Southern Highlands Research Center, Asheville

The new Bon Marche Building goes up while the Battery Park Hill is being attacked by bulldozers and the old hotel torn down. Photo courtesy The Ball Collection, Southern Highlands Research Center, Asheville

Above from the air the large leveled lot that was Battery Park Hill stretches out in front of the new Battery Park Hotel. Behind and to the right of the hotel is St. Lawrence Catholic Church with its two towers and large dome. The large building on the right is the George Vanderbilt Hotel. The old auditorium still stands beside it. The large building to the extreme left is the famous Margo Terrace Hotel. Photo courtesy Pack Memorial Library

Seeley's Castle which crowns the southern crest of Sunset Mountain with a view reaching for miles in three directions.

From material supplied to Pack Library by Mrs. Evelyn Grove Seeley in July 1951, we have the following description of the house:

"Seeley's Castle was copied from Ford Abbey (25 miles from London). The main building was constructed about 1919 with library wing addition later. Mr. Seeley was his own architect and hired draftsmen to make his plans. Italian workmen who had worked on the Grove Park Inn still lived in the neighborhood and their work gave the outer walls a tapestry-like texture. Before the castle was built on the present site, a three story rock bungalow built on two levels occupied the location, which overlooks Happy Valley (Chunn's Cove). The rocks of this bungalow were not cemented and were pulled down to give a source of material for the castle.

"The memorial windows of the castle have a meaning for the Seeley family. There is a memorial to Mr. Seeley's native state, New Jersey, Mrs. Seeley's native state, Tennessee, to Yale University (three sons) and

Asheville's Grove Park Inn built in 1913 is still regarded as one of the South's finest resort hotels. It offers a fine golf course, swimming pool, tennis courts and an excellent restaurant. In more recent years motel facilities have been built on land adjacent to the main facility. A nearby mansion now greatly enlarged, houses the WLOS—TV station. Photo courtesy The Ball Collection, Southern Highlands Research Center, Asheville

Battery Park Hill is completely
gone and the new hotel open
to the public. To the left is
Margo Terrace. An apartment
building stands on the Margo
Terrace site at the present
time. Photo courtesy The Ball
Collection, Southern Highlands Research Center, Asheville

The Grove Arcade has been
built. The office tower planned
for the top (two stories were
completed) will never be finished. It was one of the first
downtown shopping malls in
the country. Parking already
seems to be somewhat of a
problem. Photo courtesy The
Ball Collection, Southern
Highlands Research Center,
Asheville

to Smith College (daughter). The great Seal of North Carolina and our allies of World War I, France, England, United States, etc., and also President Wilson's Declaration of War are represented.

"A well balanced entrance door weighs 700 pounds and is ornamented with hand-wrought iron hardware.

"In the fireplace in the assembly room there are stones marked by copper plates from Blarney Castle and the Tower of London.

"In the library is an antique mantel, handcarved and ornamented with gold leaf with the crest of Sir Robert Peel on the left side. There was a pair of Sir Robert Peel mantels advertised in the *London Graphic*. The advertisement stated that Queen Victoria had many times been warmed by the fireside. Mr. Seeley prevailed upon the dealer to sell one of the pair and thought the mantels to be more than 100 years old and therefore did not require duty. When unpacked, a brown paper was found tucked in the back of the mantel which stated his mantel was carved by John Ashton, and information that it was 91 years old. So Mr. Seeley sent his tax money to Washington, D.C.

"The crests in the ceiling of the library are those of Mr. Seeley and the Moore family, which is Mrs. Seeley's mother's family.

"Stone lions at the entrance are Italian and had been used in Atlanta, and these were given to Mr. Seeley by his father-in-law, Dr. Edwin C. Grove. Dr. Grove widened and improved the toll road from Grove Park Inn in order to haul material for the castle. Also, Stanley Howland had a street car line which passed

Asheville High School on McDowell Street built at the height of Asheville's second "golden era" during the 1920's. The citizens of the town shook their heads when the large modern building went up, declaring it to be "impossibly far from town." Photo courtesy The Ball Collection, Southern Highlands Research Center, Asheville

the property on the way to a pavilion on Sunset Mountain, which was a favorite picnic spot for Asheville residents.''

The main part of the mansion was completed in 1919. Seeley officially called his home ''Overlook,'' but to most of the citizens of the town it was ''Seeley's Castle.''

After the Seeleys moved out of the mansion, it became the home for a number of years of the old Asheville-Biltmore College. Later the college was to move to a completely new location with newly constructed buildings, a site closer to the city. Its name was then changed to The University of North Carolina at Asheville.

Asheville has always had its share of fine homes. The Smith-McDowell home on Victoria Road, which is now being restored by the Western North Carolina Historical Association, is perhaps the oldest.

It was built around 1840 by James McConnell Smith, who married Polly Patton, daughter of Colonel John Patton. Smith built Smith's Bridge, the first prominent span across the French Broad. Later the house was owned by Major W.W. McDowell who led the ''Buncombe Riflement'' in the Civil War.

Richmond Hill, home of world traveler Richmond Pearson, sits on a high rise overlooking the French Broad River. It has somewhat fallen upon hard times in recent years, but once stood as a fine example of delicate Victorian architecture. When the house was occupied by Pearson and his sister, Miss Margorie Pearson, it was filled with rare antiques and exotic furnishings from all over the world.

The first building to stand on this site on the corner of College and Oak Streets was built in 1888 and was constructed for the Asheville Female College. The first Asheville High School was later housed in the same building. In 1916, this building was razed and the one shown went up to be used as David Millard Junior High School. Photo courtesy The Ball Collection, Southern Highlands Research Center, Asheville

Certainly one of the most unusual houses is the Hanger House at 31 Park Avenue, once known as the Ida Jolly Crawley Museum. It was built in 1876 by Peter Demons, an exile from Russia who operated a woodworking shop in Asheville. Its original cost was $33,000, which was a lot of money in those days.

It is constructed of red brick on the outside, and of the finest hardwoods to be found on the inside. The architecture is known as Russian Byzantine. What is notable is the extensive use of hand carved dark woods on the interior.

The house is open to the public by appointment only and is now owned by Howard Hanger, a jazz pianist and ordained Methodist minister.

Finis Viae (Road's End) was the name Dr. F.A. Sondley gave to his mansion at the head of Haw Creek Valley. In 1905 he bought up 400 acres and built a home that was a real show place.

Sondley was a lawyer, originally from a prestigious family of South Carolina, and in growing up had

Zealandia or "Henry's Castle" as it first looked when built on top of Beaucatcher Mountain. Later it was greatly enlarged and its style completely changed. Photo courtesy The Ball Collection, Southern Highlands Research Center, Asheville

"Ardminon" built as a private residence, was later a famous restaurant called the "Sky Club." The balconies were used for summer dining and afforded the most spectacular night views of the city. Photo courtesy The Ball Collection, Southern Highlands Research Center, Asheville

received a fine classical education. He was a great reader and collector of books with a library that contained more than 70,000 volumes, many of them rare, many first editions, all of them valuable.

Sondley was also a collector of Indian artifacts, gems and semi-precious stones, Oriental art objects and antique firearms.

Sondley was a "things" person, rather than a "people" person, which perhaps explains why he chose the then remote Haw Creek Valley for his home. Sondley, a tall, handsome man, never married and apparently had few friends. For many years of his law practice, he never used a secretary, preferring instead to write out his law briefs in his own neat, precise hand.

For the small town, Sondley certainly presented an exotic personality. His huge house constructed of stone was a hide-away, suitable for parties and great gatherings, but there were none of these.

Sondley was a prodigious writer, choosing as his subjects his state, county and town.

He left us what is undoubtedly the most complete history of Buncombe County and among his books and papers, which he left to Pack Memorial Library, there is an unpublished manuscript of perhaps three and one-half million words carefully compiled and hand written by Sondley on *The Conquest and Development of North Carolina.*

Dr. Sondley, although a remarkably brilliant lawyer who was sought out for large cases which netted him large sums of money, neverthelesss was not well known by the people of the town. Many legends sprang up about him during his lifetime. Now, perhaps he is not thought of, except by those who seek knowledge and enlightenment among the *Sondley Reference Collection* at the library.

Since 1889, another palatial home, Zealandia, has been a familiar landmark for the city. Keeping watch over the years from a site high on Beaucatcher Mountain, Zealandia has a most romantic background. Its owners have not only been people of wealth and power, but world travelers, adventurers. In 1840, J. Evans Brown from Pennsylvania began acquiring property in the area. He left the town in 1849 to go west to join with those seeking their fortunes at Sutter's Mill in the 1849 gold rush. Later Brown moved on to New Zealand where he became prominent in politics and made in a fortune in the raising of sheep. He returned to Asheville in 1884 and five years later began the construction of the castle-like home on the mountain. It was a place of unusual beauty and extensive gardens. When completed, the house was furnished in fine style with costly pieces gathered from around the world. Brown lived in the house until his death in 1895 at the age of 68.

The home then passed from the hands of the Brown family, who continued to be an important part of and to contribute greatly to the community.

In 1904, another wealthy man, Philip S. Henry, a native of Australia, came to Asheville and purchased the house for himself and his two small daughters. His young wife had recently suffered a tragic death. Henry increased the size of the house by adding a large main hall, 12 bedrooms, four bathrooms, a spacious dining room, library, loggia and carriage porch. The work was suspended temporarily when Henry went to England to work for the allies in World War I and was resumed when the family returned. Zealandia was to be the Henry family home for many years.

Henry was a lover of art and a collector. On his world travels, he had come into possession of many priceless objects, books, documents, armor and weapons, a fine collection of Remingtons and other valuable works. The collection contained such items as goblets from the banquet tables of the Incas, lamps that lit the living room of a house in Pompeii, bricks from the ancient wall of Babylon, an original manuscript of the Jewish Torah and axes used by the Crusaders.

Henry built a $70,000 art gallery and museum in 1930 near Zealandia and invited all who would to share in his appreciation of his collection. Admission to the gallery was free, and for years thousands visited and viewed the famous collection.

Many changes have taken place since those years—the gallery has been torn down and much of the property sold off. In later years Mr. and Mrs. George Dixon, who bought Zealandia as a summer home, restored much of its glory and bought back many of the art treasures.

Since it was sold by the Dixons to other owners, Zealandia has stood empty on the mountain, a silent sentinel to the comings and goings in the city below.

Many present day citizens remember the old Hamilton estate not as a private residence but as a favorite

Richmond Hill (top next page), owned by Richard Pearson, overlooked the once popular Riverside Park on the banks of the French Broad River. The park was completely destroyed in the flood of 1916 which caused sweeping damage to Asheville. Photo by Lou Harshaw

The Gudger Home (at right) on Montford is being restored by the Preservation Society of Asheville and Buncombe County and the Montford Community Club. Photo by Lou Harshaw

Dr. Carl Von Ruck combined two imposing structures on Von Ruck Terrace for his home. He came to the city to treat "lung disease" during the time of Asheville's fame as a health resort. This structure is now an apartment house. Photo by Lou Harshaw

nightclub, appropriately called the Sky Club. The stately home, empty and lonesome, sits on Beaucatcher Mountain affording what is probably the finest view overlooking Asheville. It gained fame far and wide for its excellent food and nighttime spectacular of the lighted city.

The three storied stone residence was called Ardminon by Mr. and Mrs. O.C. Hamilton when they lived there. They came to the city in 1896 and bought up 115 acres on the mountain.

From a quarry on the property came stone for several buildings—the main Hamilton house, the stable which is now ivy covered, some of the houses on Carroll Avenue, and two apartment houses on Biltmore Avenue which the Hamiltons owned at that time.

One of the most distinguishing features of the house is the broad porch with its two balconies above, supported by stone columns.

An exquisite old house on Zillicon Avenue has, in more recent years, gained a new life as the Administration Building of Highland Hospital. It was called Hopewell Hall when it was built in 1896 by John G.

Baker for his daughter, Martha Elizabeth, as a wedding present. She was married to James Edwin Rumbough and they had one son, John Baker Rumbough.

Rumbough lived in the house until he died in April of 1941 at the age of 80. After that, members of the family lived in the mansion for several years.

Another large home, that of Dr. Robert S. Carroll, a pioneer in psychiatric medicine, is next door to the Rumbough house and serves as a school for patients of the hospital.

The Carroll and Rumbough homes were originally a part of the Montford area, which has been designated a National Historic District.

Montford Park was Asheville's first major real estate development and dates from the boom period of the late 1800's to about 1920. Most of Asheville's leading families, including that of Locke Craig who in 1912 was elected governor of the state, lived in the park. Many of the houses were designed by architect Richard Sharpe Smith, and part of their charm is that they vary greatly in style and interpretation.

In recent years, two groups, the Preservation Society of Asheville and Buncombe County and The Montford Community Club, have been responsible for much of the interest in the rehabilitation of the Montford area. The Preservation Society has acquired the Gudger House at 89 Montford, donated by First Federal Savings and Loan of Hendersonville, and is restoring the property.

Another group, Historic Montford, Inc., composed of 30 to 40 members (mostly young people), have undertaken the rehabilitation of a number of houses in this residential district. They have established a hummingbird insignia for display and publish a newsletter.

Many of the palatial homes of early Asheville are now long gone, remembered only in the yellowed and finger-worn newspaper clippings from other times in other years.

During the second boom in the twenties, new residential developments sprang up around the city as fast as steam rollers could move in to lay out streets. The dam was built for Beaver Lake and the surrounding area designated Lakeview Park. Kenilworth had been started a bit earlier and was fairly well built up with family homes of the upper middle income bracket. But Lakeview Park was to be a grand affair with huge mansions to be situated on large lots, surrounded either by high walls or tall ironwork fences. The promotional folders portrayed elegance and architectural distinction as the hallmark at Lakeview Park.

Malvern Hills, another neighborhood of grace and beauty, was laid out in West Asheville and a few large homes went in.

Out in the country, very far out in the country it seemed at the time, Royal Pines residential section was surveyed on and around Mt. Royal. East of the city, land for Beverly Hills was quickly bought up and a new residential section planned. It was here along the border of Beverly Hills that Asheville opened the first nine holes of a municipal golf course. The other nine holes would be opened in 1927.

The competition became fierce; land devlopers and real estate sales people flocked into the mountain city from the waning Florida real estate boom. Sometimes it seemed as if their offices were set up on the street corners and park benches, where some of the bolder souls hawked and shouted their wares like carnival barkers "working the crowd." The printers were kept busy night and day, turning out brochures extolling the virtues of the new real estate ventures. Every train was met with free tours offered to the more prosperous looking of the tourists.

Not all of the visitors to Asheville could afford to stay at the luxurious hotels, so many thriving "tourist homes" opened up in the city. Mostly these were private homes built with many bedrooms to house large families, but now taken over by a couple who lived in the house and rented rooms, or sometimes a widow left with a big house and little money who could enter the genteel trade of letting rooms by the week or by the night.

It was one of these, a rambling wooden house that was painted white and situated on Spruce Street, which was bought in 1907 by Mrs. W.O. Wolfe. This house was to become, modest as it was, one of the most famous boarding houses in the world. Mrs. Wolfe called her boarding establishment "The Old Kentucky Home." The purchase of the house by Mrs. Wolfe and her subsequent running of it was to split the Wolfe family into factions. The writings of her son Tom about life in the house and the town in general was to divide its citizenship in a cleavage that was to last many bitter years.

So, in the hectic mad pace of business expansion, the wild flurry of the "paper profits" mounting ever higher, another storm was brewing in the form of a book. Tom Wolfe's novel *Look Homeward Angel* would rock the town on its moral foundations. The rapid and almost total failures of the business world would deal it a near fatal blow financially.

Many milestones had been marked in the period of prosperity. The prestigious Asheville School for Boys, west of town, had been founded. The next year the city limits were expanded, and in 1902 an auditiorium was built on Haywood Street.

Wachovia Bank and Trust Company opened a branch in the city.

In 1906 The Citizens Bank opened. That same year Dr. L.M. McCormick, Asheville city bacteriologist, began his "swat the fly" campaign. This was in line with the growing reputation of the city as a health center. The campaign was the first of its kind in the country and attracted national attention. Asheville doctors were writing articles for national health publications on the benefits of the clean air, mild climate and pure water of the southern mountains. A good part of the growth could be attributed to the increasing number of excellent health facilities being built.

The first large industry, Champion Paper and Fibre Company, came to the small town of Canton, west of Asheville, in 1907. In 1908, still another goup with special interests started a trend which has continued to expand and have impact in the area—the Southern Baptists opened Ridgecrest Assembly. The Methodists settled at Lake Junaluska a few years later. The Presbyterians settled at Montreat for their southern meetings.

The population had grown to 18,762.

Asheville, tentatively, hestiatingly, made its entrance into the air age when, in 1912, Lincoln Beachey shipped the first airplane to enter the city in on a flat bed car. After flying over the area for a few minutes, Beachey brought the plane down and announced that the mountain currents were too tricky to do any flying here.

It remained for Henry Westall to actually fly the first airplane into town. He landed his OX5 powered Jenny in Baird Bottoms, the area now covered by Beaver Lake. Baird Bottoms was not used long as a "flying field" because of the continuous cross winds blowing through the valley.

Scott Dillingham and Worth Lyerly bought Westall's plane in 1920 and used a corn field in the Haw Creek section as a landing field.

Dr. J.E. Owen, an Asheville dentist, became one of the first serious pioneers of flying in the mountains.

Owen, along with Tally J. Roberts, Ed Buyck and Luther Johnson, took over part of the Carrier Field in West Asheville and spent many years flying early model planes in and out of Asheville.

For a fee they would take the more daring souls for a Sunday afternoon ride over the town.

Joe Bly, nephew of Owen and now information officer for the Asheville Post Office, remembers that his uncle used to atract the crowds by taking up a glider and sailing over the area as a sort of advertisement for business.

Bly, just a lad at the time, would move among the potential passengers selling cold drinks. It was also

Spruce Street looking toward the new (and first) Asheville "Skyscraper," the Jackson Building. The City Hall and fire station building have been torn down making way for the City-County Plaza and the new municipal building. The imposing structure in the center is the new medical building. Photo courtesy The Ball Collection, Southern Highlands Research Center, Asheville

The Auditorium built by the Public Works Administration
during the depression was to be rebuilt yet again and greatly
expanded for conventions, sports and other spectator events.
In the background the Asheville Bypass, highway connector
No. 240, is taking shape. The battle over the highway "cut"
through Beaucatcher Mountain is yet to come. Photo courtesy Pack Memorial Library

one of his duties to pump the gas, red in color and pumped from the old fashioned pump with the huge glass dome on top into which the gas traveled first in order for the customer to see he was receiving the correct amount. From there it was hosed into the plane. It was all an exciting and thrilling adventure for young Joe Bly, and the most adventurous thing of all was the occasional airplane ride he was able to talk his uncle into giving him.

The next airfield was the old Asheville-Hendersonville Airport which handled a number of United commercial flights. With advancing air technology in instrument and night flying, the facility soon became obsolete.

On May 14, 1957, the citizens of Asheville voted to approve the construction of the present airport facility.

Nature chose the year of 1916 to bring to the city the greatest tragedy in its history up to the present time. Death and destruction came with the flooding of the French Broad River. It swept through tiny Biltmore Village to claim lives and property. But unquestionably the greatest property loss was beautiful Riverside Park, a fashionable gathering place for young and old of the city. The Park lay along the banks of the river on the northern side. Crowning the rise above it was the Pearson home, Richmond Hill. When the waters receded, the Park was in total ruins. The flood sealed its fate, for it was never to be rebuilt.

Asheville city limits expanded to take in West Asheville in 1917.

As the first great war in Europe began to draw to a close, the economic forces at home were swirling ever and ever faster. The U.S. Government built the large Oteen Hospital in 1918, and servicemen came back to the mountains to find a city greatly changed. It was to change even more in the next few years.

The new Battery Park Hotel opened in 1924, as did the new George Vanderbilt Hotel a block away. The city fire department was established on a full time operation during this year, and Asheville's first skyscraper went up—the Jackson Building, delicately styled, slim and handsomely decorated. Its builder, L.B. Jackson, sought large profits from the Asheville business boom.

In 1925, the Asheville Biltmore Hotel opened its doors.

Up in Washington, in 1929, events were taking place which would in time alter the entire profile and economic outlook of western North Carolina. Congress authorized a national park in the Great Smoky Mountains. It would take many years to come to fruition, and many more before the Park would begin to have an economic impact on Asheville.

American Enka began buying up land in Hominy Valley in 1927. They would construct a huge rayon plant. This was a project that had an immediate effect—first the purchase of the lands and the hiring of local workers for the construction, and later permanent employment.

By 1928, most of the residential sections in or close to the business section had been filled. The more wealthy and fashionable crowd over the years and generations had gradually shifted into new areas as they do with any expanding town. Some of the first ornate large homes were built on a high rise at the outer western rim of the city, overlooking the French Broad River which included Park Avenue, the town's first street of style. From this section high fashion homes went in on Chestnut Street, then perhaps South French Broad and Aston Park were considered the "best" place to live. Montford was developed soon after these.

The year of 1928 was the high point in the city's history as far as construction is concerned. It was the peak year of the boom. We can imagine that the gala celebrations and ribbon cuttings came on fast upon one another.

Among the public buildings opened were Asheville's new City Hall and the Buncombe County Courthouse bordering the Court Plaza. The new senior high school, an impressive building on McDowell, was completed as was Beaucatcher Tunnel and McDowell Street viaduct. The Rhododendron Festival was inaugurated in Asheville, an annual event including a number of parades, parties, dances, and pageants over a period of a week in June. The Rhododendren Festival heralded the beginning of modern tourism in the mountain metropolis and did more than any project to make Asheville known to the new generation who made automobiles their mode of travel. Automobiles were to change the travel and resort industry as drastically from the days of the private train car and Pullman Coach as trains had altered travel from the time of the stage coach and covered wagon. Yet to come, of course, was the age of commercial air traffic and the changes it would bring. In fact, in the same busy year of 1928, a site was selected on the southside of Asheville to construct an airport.

The age of Art Deco had arrived in the city by 1928. The new Post Office at the corner of Post and Otis Streets opened the following year would be a fine example.

By the 1920's, Asheville's Art Deco period had begun. The new City Building was something citizens could point to with pride. Photo courtesy The Ball Collection, Southern Highlands Research Center, Asheville

By the end of this year the population had grown to 50,193. On the surface Asheville was an extremely prosperous town expanding rapidly in all directions, but in reality business interests not only in Asheville, but all over the world, were on the edge of precipice. Some would see the abyss yawning widely before them and would take steps to withdraw from the edge. But with paper profits climbing ever higher, not many would foresee the dangers.

On November 20, 1930, Asheville's Central Bank and Trust Company, the largest financial institution in Western North Carolina, failed to open its doors to the public at the appointed hour. Nor were they to open for business again. As it went under, so did five other banks and a number of insurance and trust associations.

It would not only be the wealthy who lost heavily. The losses would filter down through all levels. Small businesses would take a loss and close. The elderly would find their life savings gone. Homes, lived in a generation or more, would go. It was a tragedy of unprecedented proportions, a tragedy the magnitude of its kind never before experienced in this country. Almost all of Asheville's financial system would collapse.

In West Asheville, a middle class community, women, housewives, threw their coats over their cotton housedresses, grasped their children by the hand and walked to the Central Bank on Haywood Road. There in the pale morning light they huddled together on the sidewalk, the children fidgety and fearful. Some of the women beat on the doors, calling for those inside to open the bank. Some cried. Eventually around noon when the children began to get hungry and complain, they dispersed and went back to their homes. Even in those hours the cloak of hopelessness was settling over their shoulders. It would be days, weeks even, before the full extent of the damage would be known.

Uptown, there would be suicides as there would be all over the country.

The bottom line for city and county loss of public funds would be over eight million dollars. Almost nothing would be recovered from their bank deposits.

All over the country, municipalities were declaring bankruptcy. The town and county didn't take the easy way out. The civic leaders decided that the only honorable course was to repay their debts. This was to put the town in hock for 40 years. The economy would grind down and come to a halt. Only occasionally would it stir to life. Almost no new buildings would go up. Downtown Asheville would be contained within its 1930 boundaries for some 15 years.

Out in the new suburbs, so lately areas of so much promise, the randomly built residential structures, home of the prestigious and well-to-do, capped off the best lying lots. In hilly country these are always the first to be utilized. The houses would stand lonesomely and alone, sometimes without tenants. In Lakeview Park large areas of wilderness would separate the residences, and it would be the same in Royal PInes, Malvern Hills and Beverly Hills.

A period of stagnation was upon the town, and yet a few brave community leaders accepted it as their duty to get together and work out a plan which would answer their moral obligations concerning the huge civic debt Asheville owed. The plan they worked out was comprehensive and long range. It would become known as the "Sinking Fund," with a Sinking Fund Commission to oversee its operation. We can only speculate that its planners gave little thought that the debts, a retirement of $48,256,912.71 would be completed in the year 1976 when, of course, another great celebration involving the entire community would be due to be held.

In a series of articles written for *The Asheville Citizen Times* in 1964, Doug Reed states: "The settlement of public debts of Asheville and Buncombe County in 1936 was both generous and exacting. It was generous in that it forgave unpaid interest in default and greatly reduced furture interest rates. It was exacting in that it was binding. It left no area for further manipulation of the legal indebtedness. It left no option but to pay the bills.

"Thus, the 1936 debt settlement was to have no mere influence in shaping the pattern of development of the metropolitan community. More than any other single thing, this was the dominant reality—and still is—that controls the growth of Asheville and Buncombe County."

Those who would crowd into the Thomas Wolfe Auditorium to celebrate the retirement of Asheville's depression debt would be mostly new faces, free at last to move ahead with assurance and confidence once more.

To paraphrase John F. Kennedy, the torch had been passed.

The author William Sydney Porter who wrote short stories under the pseudonym of "O. Henry" lived in Asheville and married an Asheville girl, Sara Coleman Porter. Porter and his wife are buried in Riverside Cemetery. Photo by Lou Harshaw

Asheville's first auditorium. It sat on the same site as today's large civic center. This auditorium burned and was replaced by one built during the depression by the Public Works Administration. Photo courtesy Pack Memorial Library

*A look up Church Street toward Patton Avenue. Directly
ahead is the M.V. Moore Department Store, later to burn to
the ground, and the crenellated tower on top of the Drhumor
Building may be seen. Photo courtesy The Ball Collection,
Southern Highlands Research Center, Asheville*

Haywood Street. The large building in the foreground is the Miles Building. The empty space where the building materials are stacked will soon become the new Bon Marche building, then, later, the home of Ivey's Department Store. The building now houses the Money Tree. This intersection had not yet become busy enough for a "red" light. Photo courtesy The Ball Collection, Southern Highlands Research Center, Asheville

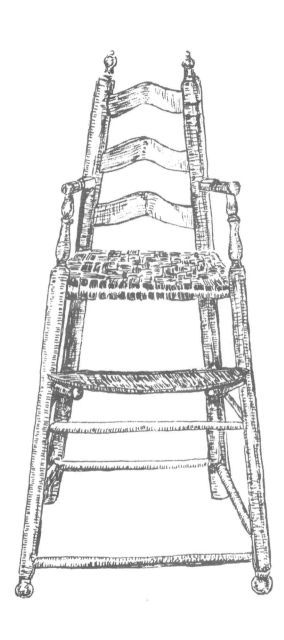

CHAPTER VII

Someone To Be Proud Of

WITHIN the lifetime of the writer two people just before dying, have come to say their farewells to me. Seemingly, both of these people had a premonition that they would not be back.

The first was C.R. Sumner. He was very ill and due to make a third trip to one of the large hospitals in the North for a major, critical operation. He came into my office late one afternoon as he sometimes did, just for a chat. Then he told me that he had come because he wouldn't make it back. He was so brave, I couldn't let him see my sadness.

At his gentle request, I left my office in the City Hall that afternoon and strolled back across town with him. He talked of some of the things he had tried to do over the years, of his teaching, creative writing and drama classes, in the small nearby college where I first met him when I was a student. He had always encouraged us all, to write, to act, to go forth and try to discover whatever talents we might possess. He talked of his work as an artist and how much pleasure this hobby had given him. But most of all he talked of his years on the newspaper as a reporter, some of the people he had known, some of the things he disapproved of in the town, but how very much he loved it.

It was a poignant moment between the teacher and the former pupil as we paused before the newspaper office building in the gathering dusk. He asked if I minded the walk alone back across town. I told him no. Then we formally shook hands. Before he turned away he asked me to remember him because this would be the last time we would see each other, and it was.

The other person who came to say goodbye to me just before her death was Mabel Wolfe Wheaton, sister of author Thomas Wolfe. She liked me and I liked her. We could communicate, Mabel and I.

I had helped in her efforts and those of the Wolfe family to get the Wolfe boardinghouse on Spruce Street transferred into the hands of the city fathers and to get the outstanding debts paid so that "Old Kentucky Home" or "Dixieland" as Tom called it in his book, *Look Homeward Angel*, might be permanently preserved as a memorial. Now Mabel was ill and although still looking well, she somehow knew that she would not return to Asheville when she went away for a second operation. She wanted to say goodbye, she said. I, too, knew that as well as Mabel looked, this would be the last time I would see her. She was also very fond of my boss, Richard K. Degenhardt, Executive Vice President of the Asheville Chamber of Commerce, and asked if we could go around to his office. He took her hand and told her lightly he didn't believe her—that he was sure everything would be fine, but Mabel wasn't having any of that. She said there were some things she wanted us to do for her. She wanted us to go to the house and speak to Ralph, her husband, when we received the word that she was gone, and she wanted us to speak to Fred, her brother.

115

Mabel Wolfe Wheaton, sister of author Thomas Wolfe, as a young woman. Photo courtesy Pack memorial Library

She wanted us to try to keep an eye on the Memorial, the old boarding house, if we could do that, and then she thanked us for all we had done for the family. We, she and I, walked slowly back to my office, talking for the last time about last things. She mentioned that she guessed she'd never write a book, although after Tom had become so famous she had wanted to. She rather touchingly told me she knew Tom would always be rememberd, but she didn't guess she would.

(Note: In 1961 Legette Blythe working with Mabel as co-author, using for the most part notes and recordings researched after her death, wrote a book entitled *Thomas Wolfe and His Family*, published by Doubleday and Co.)

To me Mabel Wolfe Wheaton had always seemed a rather heroic figure, large in size, a rather exaggerated personality, a staunch supporter of, and deeply loyal to, all the Wolfe family, she especially loved Tom.

Mabel was right, just as Mr. Sumner had been.

In a short week and a half, I believe it was, she was gone.

Not too many months before her last visit Mabel had come by the office and we had gone together to the radio station where my husband was on duty. We sat together while Mabel talked about her family, recording on tape, her memories of the life they lived in Asheville. She wanted to recall Tom and preserve her memories of him.

Several paragraphs from the tapes were used by the National Broadcasting Company in their radio series *Biographies In Sound*. Other than that, as far as I know, the tapes have never been printed before.

The reminiscences that follow are not my writing. They are not the written words of Mabel Wolfe Wheaton. They are her spoken words, just as her thoughts came to her.

I have done some editing, but because the natural flow of her narrative reflects Mabel's personality so well, I have tried to preserve as much as possible, her thoughts just as they came to her. Since Tom Wolfe is one of this country's most outstanding, most respected authors and since his books have been translated into many languages and read in almost every country in the world, I have included the transcript almost in its entirety.

(Note: Some of the members of Mabel's family have passed on since this tape was recorded.)

So here, Mabel, are your "memories" just as you told them to me so long ago:

"I am Mabel Wolfe Wheaton, sister of Thomas Wolfe.

"I want to tell you a little about those who are living today in our family. Our sister Effie who was living at the time of Tom's death, passed away five years ago from a stroke. She left a family of seven. One of the family died two months ago, with a cerebral hemorrhage in Washington, D.C. Died quite suddenly, Fredericka Gamble Gennett.

"Our brother Frank, he's the oldest of the family. Frank is very ill in a sanatorium here in Asheville. He has an arthritic trouble but it's broken down everything and he seldom leaves his bed. He's nearly 67 years old. Frank has a son in New Albany, Indiana who is a doctor. Dr. Deats Wolfe and Deats has three sons. The oldest is Thomas Clayton Wolfe, namesake of Tom and they're doing quite well.

"I have, of course, this brother who went through it all and who has always been grand and glorious to us all and has been certainly the mainstay to depend on since our father's death. This is Fred, who lives at Spartanburg. He is married. He and Mary live there on Oatis Boulevard. They have no children.

"Ralph and I came two years ago back to Asheville and we have no children. Fred comes here quite often to see us. Fred and Mary and Frank, of course, we go to see him a couple of times a week, sometimes oftener.

"I want to pay tribute to our parents. I don't think we appreciate parents until we are old ourselves and think back. I always thought mine were pretty wonderful. Mama and I were not as much in tune in my early days as my father and I. I thought he was just the finest person living, and the strongest and the bravest. And I could depend on his judgment. Papa was well read. He didn't have the formal education but when he married Mama, he read books like Shakespeare and Dickens and all Dickens, and the Waverly Novels and *The Factory* and Chambers' *Encyclopedia*. And he had all the poets and all the poets he could buy. He loved poetry. And these great orations in the books by Shakespeare like Hamlet's *Soliloquy* and Portia's speech and he loved the opera *Othello*. I mean he loved the book *Othello*, is what I'm trying to say. He loved the story. And he could quote all those things. I think back now, how we would, to please him and to get a little preference, to get a little brag, in other words, we'd learn what he liked.

"When I was just a little girl, he'd stand me up to recite. He knew 'The Raven' and Grey's 'Eulogy,' all the way through and when Tom went to Mama's house, when she bought this boarding house in 1907, she more or less left us. She was busy with her boarders.

"Tom was seven years old and from that time on he became more of a companion of Papa, especially after Bennie's death in 1918. And Tom would go to picture shows with Papa. Tom would read with Papa in the evening. He would lie on the floor before the big sitting room fire at our old home place and they read the same books. I think Tom's brain would ask questions and was matured to some extent as much as our Father's then.

"But he would pull down these books of Thackery, you know Scott and the poets and Milton's *Paradise Lost*. And I think we had the best library in that part of the town because when I was writing my little compostions in high school, most of my friends gathered at our house to refer to things, to get reference and nothing pleased Papa more than to see the need of his presence so he could look it up for us and find out about these things.

"And my mother was a school teacher, she grew up in the hills here of North Carolina, from a very good, fine old family the Westalls, whose beginning seems to be, as far as I know, English and Scotch. Her father, Westall, always told us of his ancestors from England and her mother was named Penland. And many of them are around Burnsville, N.C. Mama moved then into Swannanoa. Swannanoa is a little town near Asheville out here around sixteen miles. A beautiful place and the old place where the family lived is still standing. Mama went to teaching in Mitchell County over here. I got her organ back for the house, for the Memorial just a year ago. And Mama went to teaching in the summer time when she didn't get too much she'd come home to her people who lived here in Asheville at the time and then she'd sell books. And she met my father selling books.

"He saw her coming acorss the Public Square and he'd lost his wife just a few months before. His other wife Cynthia, who's buried in the same plot of ground as my mother, and all the rest, Tom and Ben, and all of them. And we just adored Cynthia. We'd heard him talk so much about her that we just thought she belonged to us too. She was the wife before.

"But Mama came across the square and some man of the town who read a great deal had sent her in to see this old widower from the North. This man who had come from the North with a wife, who read all the time.

"So Mama went in and he thought she was just the prettiest little thing he'd ever seen. He said she was as pretty as a pigeon, whatever that means. And he said she came in and he said Mama always had business or the desire to have more than the mountain country gave her, the things of life, money, that could get them. And she said, 'How's business? You're doing pretty well here, now aren't you?' And presently she opened this thing which he saw was a prospectus and he said 'Merciful God, a book agent.' And then she sold him the book, called *The Golden Treasury of Poetry and Prose*. He loved it all of his life. Then they were married, probably nine months later.

"But Mama had the school training. She didn't have time with all of us children to sit around, she sewed in the evenings. She didn't have the time to read as much as our father did. And probably was more dramatic and more of an extrovert. We had all that. We inherited all that. But I realize now when I think of Tom and then I think of some of the wonderful qualities of the others, I think we got them from our parents. I think the combination of the two, I think Mama's sticking to things until success came or to the end always, and Papa's great desire and his enthusiasm for life and enthusiasm, his love of good things.

"He carved you know, in marble. He had marble bibles, door stops, marble card trays, calling card trays and things that he made out of scraps of marble that were perfectly beautiful. I think Papa's love of all that certainly helped Tom.

"Now, today at Asheville, Mama's old boarding house, which was the 'Old Kentucky Home,' which we, before the end of things, we loathed. And which Tom called in his books 'Dixieland.' He made it famous, was bought a few years ago by a group and it's now the Thomas Wolfe Memorial. All the things in the house they're all authentic. We've tried to keep it, I've tried to help them keep it in order and keep it clean. All the family pictures are there on the wall. The place looks very well.

"The old dining room is set up with the tables. The dining room as I, I was married in that dining room 39 years ago. It held about 40 people comfortably and 50 if you crowded them at little tables. And it's all set up with the dishes there. The old kitchen, the old stove and the equipment she had for meals is in the kitchen there. And Tom's New York furniture, the furniture he lived with when he wrote his last book was shipped home and there is a room fixed up upstairs with that. And in another room the furniture that was in the bedroom when my mother married my father and her family began coming along, the bed that we were all born on and the other furniture everything is there.

"I want to tell you a little of Tom's birth into our family and a little of our background and a few of the memories of him as a child.

"Tom was born in the family Oct. 3, 1900. He was born at 92 Woodfin Street, Asheville, North Carolina. We were born in the same room; a family of eight. People didn't throw their furniture away in those days so the house had set there for years, about as it started.

"Tom was a very good baby. He came along six years after Fred, and was a child of our parents' old age and they expected great things out of him. He was so good, he didn't cry, he didn't make any noise. There was a long laundry basket brought in from the backyard and placed on a trunk, one of those old storage trunks, in Mama's room near the fireplace. That was padded and was Tom's cradle. You didn't hear a sound out of him in the day time. We'd go there and tickle him or nudge him or something and he'd ooh up at us, but he never cried.

"Shortly, it must have been in the spring, following his birth in October, that Mama early one spring morning said 'I'm going downtown. I'm going to leave all of you here to look after things. You aren't coming along. You're going to stay here and look after things, the cooking and everything.' She went through the hall, we following her, on her way up to dress and we heard the cooing of the baby, 'coo, coo, coo.' And she turned around to us and she said, 'Well, I'll declare, I'll declare, I got a baby. I forgot all about it.' He was just that good.

"Well, along about nine months after his birth, along in the spring, I remember father taking him out in the backyard. He had all kinds of fruit trees in bloom, apples, cherry, pears, plums and the grapes on the vines in the arbor and every square foot of that backyard, 360 feet deep, covered with vegetables or fruit to feed the family. And Papa would go out early, sometimes six and seven o'clock in the morning to look over his garden and look over the fruit trees and on this occasion he took Tom and went to the backyard. And I think we'd looked at him and wondered if he'd ever talk, or if he'd ever make a sound. But when he got to the backyard there was a cow on the other side of the fence, way at the rear belonging to the Britt family. Mr. Britt went to Congress. James A. Britt was one of our congressmen. But this cow belonged to them and the cow leaned over the fence and the cow said, 'Moo.' And Tom immediately looked and looked at our father and he said 'Moo.'

"Papa was so delighted with it all that he came bounding in and he came up the back stairway and he said, 'Julia, Julia, he said, he said, "Moo." ' And she said, 'Oh, you crazy thing, you fool you, go on, of course he'll talk.'

"Well, he came along. He stood on the floor and played with blocks and played with books the older one's of us had had. And we'd go to town and we had a little money and we'd buy him a plaything and teach him what was written underneath it. And he didn't know how to read, but we'd say this said this in explanation and pretty soon, even if it were upside down when the neighbors would come in or relatives, to show him off my father would say, 'Read it to them, Tom.' And he could read it perfectly. He just memorized it.

"And when he was five years old, he played with the neighborhood boys, Max Israel and Charles Perkinson and Max had to start to school. It was the law of the town to go to school at six, and Max was just one year older than Tom. A little more perhaps. But he started to school and Tom was lost knowing Max wouldn't be with him, and so Mama said, 'I looked down the street and I saw Tom look back at me and I knew I'd lost my baby.' He was just past five years but he insisted on going to school with Max Israel. He went for several days. And when she thought she'd have to keep him at home, the teacher said, 'Oh, let him come on, he's doing just as well as the others.' And so he was kept on at the school. He seemed to be fond of, and to like the history of the world and travel and literature but he was no good at handwriting. I know they tried to teach him in his copybook to write. It was just hieroglyphics, you couldn't tell and this Max Israel, he said, 'Oh shaw, it isn't writing.' And he could write beautifully right under it all and so Tom rather than be outdone why he began writing that morning. He made a pretty good go of it in the copybook.

"But he came along in the years of his childhood and Mama would take him out of school and he was tripping around the country going to Florida every year or down to New Orleans to the Mardi Gras or out to visit someone of the family. Frank was living in Louisville and she would take Tom out because he could go on a half ticket. It worried the family worried Papa particularly, that the boy was being taken out of school.

"On one occasion when Tom was just 12 years old, 1912, she took him up to Washington, D.C. for the inauguration of Woodrow Wilson. Papa was a strong Republican and had come from Pennsylvania to the mountains and he voted a straight Republican ticket. Mama being born here, a native, she was a straight Democrat and voted a Democratic ticket when suffrage came in.

"But on this occasion, when she went to Washington to see the inauguration, they stopped over someplace near the capitol in one of those rooming houses and the morning of the big parade, the inaugural parade, why she took him to some restaurant and she said, 'Now, child, just eat all you can.' And there was bread always brought, piles of bread those days to the table, and she said, 'Take all the bread you can.' He put the bread in his waist and they walked all the way that day from the Capitol to the White House. They saw everything and when he came home he told the story about eating this bread and being kept on his feet all day and not going near food and not being near a place to rest and our father was just furious. He didn't like Woodrow Wilson in the beginning of his presidency because nothing in the world except he was Republican. He said to her he said 'Woman' —he would speak always to our mother when he would get serious, he would always say, 'Woman, you took that child to Washington, you starved him, you made him walk that long drive to see that miserable scoundrel inaugurated. You ought to be standing on your head eating grass before his reign is over.' And so, those were some of the furious moments in our childhood days. Those fights and conflicts between them over things of that kind.

"Tom was 12 years old when he entered the North State School. He had been in the public schools and the last year of his going to the public schools (I think it was 7th grade), a man by the name of J.M. Roberts was the principal of the school. Mr. Roberts was a very good principal. He only stayed there one year but his idea was to get up a private school.

"Mrs. Roberts, Tom's old teacher who has been known as his beloved Margaret, in his books and everything, Margaret Roberts, didn't know Tom when he was in public schools. But Mr. Roberts wrote a little story, a little French story and he asked the grades, the three grades, I think it was the 6th, 7th and 8th, to write a little essay on what they remembered of his reading. He read them the story and he wanted their interpretation or their review of the thing. And they all wrote.

"Up until that time I don't think he paid special attention to Tom Wolfe, except that he got good grades. He took these little compositions home and Mrs. Roberts was to look them over in her spare time. She wasn't teaching. And she said to Mr. Roberts a few days later, 'Who is this Tom Wolfe?' And he said, 'Well, he lives over here on Woodfin Street. His father is in the tombstone business down on the Square, in the monument business.' She said, 'Well, this is the best one of them all.'

"Then it was that Mr. Roberts entreated Tom to join his crowd for the private school. Well, a private school was something new in our family. Our father was a large taxpayer in the little town and he felt that we should exhaust all the facilities of the public schools. None of the older ones had ever been in a private school until they had either graduated from the public school or had been kicked out, we might say, or something and then perhaps the private school came in.

"But Tom at that age doing so well in the public schools and ahead of his classes all the time, Papa saw no necessity for a private school. But Tom and Mr. Roberts went to Mama first. Of course, Tom was her baby, and she was all for it but she said, 'You'll have to go up and speak to Mr. Wolfe.' She always called our father Mr. Wolfe, always. And she said, 'Talk to him about it. He'll have it to pay so go up and talk to him.' So Tom and Mr. Roberts went to Papa's shop on the Square and Papa, of course, roamed around and couldn't see the reason but he finally turned to Mr. Roberts and he said, 'Does the boy work?' Mr. Roberts told him that he was at the head of his classes and he couldn't do nearly as well in a large group as he could with private teachers. So, Papa said, 'If the boy wants it, he shall have it.' So Tom went to Mr. Roberts' school. They called it in the beginning the North State School and he was there for a year.

"He, of course, became their outstanding pupil and the night he graduated from the private

Author Thomas Wolfe as a child. His mother had not yet cut his long curls. Photo courtesy Pack Memorial Library

school, he had taken nearly all the medals during the week. And Tom bounded out on the lawn where I was with my fiancé. I was married that month, this was in June 1916 and I was married on the 28th. I can't give the the date of the graduation from the private school, but it was just a week or so earlier. And he bounded out to us on the lawn, we couldn't get in the house. They were hanging from the windows and all around they crowded into these large rooms. But we could hear Tom's booming voice outside. We also heard a young man who was one of their pupils, Jack Cheesborough, who is a lawyer here in Asheville now. And Jack's essay—we thought it quite good. But Jack's wasn't the big booming voice of Tom Wolfe and Tom came out and he caught hold of me and he said, 'His speech was just as good as mine, his speech was just as good as mine. The only reason I won was my voice. I have a bigger voice.' And of course, this fog horn voice of Tom's did win. Well, that was 1916. He was only 15 years old; he was 16 in the fall.

"I want to tell you though, digressing a little from the subject. Mama bought 'The Old Kentucky Home' in 1907. Tom was seven years old in October following, in 1907, Oct. 3rd, he was seven years old. He went to the house, it was just a block and a half from our old home. We older children stayed at our home with our father. But she took Tom her baby. She thought he belonged with her and the rest of us could live down at the other place. In fact it took two houses to keep boarders and keep the family, too. And Tom, we thought the boarding house was wonderful the first night we went there. Boarders were all right. Boarding house was all right. There were servants, three servants. Our tables, the tables in the old dining room, which seated about 50, were made long, seating eight and ten. And our table was close to the hall door as you entered. And we thought it was fine. But when the family began to stay down at the old home place for their meals, because papa didn't like boarding houses, and Tom had to stay up there, he resented it. And he came down to us as often as he could. But we, on most night occasions would have dinner up at the house there in those days. And Mama would close it in the winter and take Tom with her down to St. Petersburg, Florida or to Palm Beach. They were gone for three months. And he got to see a little of the country. He was in Miami, St. Petersburg, Daytona, Clearwater and once they went to Hot Springs, Arkansas.

"I remember when they left the Asheville Station a little incident. I was about 19 and Tom was 9 years old and we were weeping, too, to say goodbye to them. And he looked at me and said, 'Don't cry, Mabel, it'll be all over by the time I get to Morristown.' Morristown is down here around 60 miles and he knew if we were separated one hour other things would take our thoughts and there wouldn't be much weeping.

"Well, I was married the 28th of June, 1916, in the 'Old Kentucky Home,' which is now the 'Dixieland' of Tom's novel and known as the Thomas Wolfe Memorial today. But Tom, I think, made it famous by calling it 'Dixieland' in his books and I was married there the 28th of June and went to Raleigh to live.

"Tom had wanted to go to the University of Virginia, but our father wanted to make a lawyer of him. And he knew that his tuition and everything would be cheaper in the State University. And he thought his contacts would be better took being in his own state, if he were to practice law here in the state. But Tom had other ideas. No one knew he intended to be a writer. We thought a lawyer with his big voice and his command of the English when he was a great speaker. He could get up at any moment in school and seem to have possession of his faculties and could think on his feet.

"And of course, Father would say, kept saying to us, 'Don't you laugh.' Tom was you know, just the sun, moon and stars to them when he was a child. And he said, 'Don't you laugh at him. He'll be governor of the state some day. He'll go to the United States Senate.' We didn't know about the writing part, of course. We knew that he had done well in his little essays at school, his little competitions.

"So he went down to the University in September. I have letters and they'll be brought out in the Book of Letters where he wrote notes to my husband and asked him to meet him. We were living in Raleigh which was thirty miles away from Chapel Hill which is where the state university is. And he wrote to meet him and to go over with him and make the business arrangement. So Tom entered that fall at Chapel Hill. The first year I lived in Raleigh and he came often to see me. I remember he writes in the book, the fictional part of his going to the football game at Richmond, Va. This was 1916 in the fall of 1916, when they had football games at the University. The University of N.C. played Virginia at Richmond, I believe. And for nine or ten years, probably longer,

Virginia had won every year. But on this occasion this game was to be at Richmond again. And I had been written to meet Tom at Raleigh to take him home with me for Thanksgiving dinner the next day. And we got to the train. I was very much opposed to it. I thought what do I have to have, I'm a bride and I want to be alone and go where we want to tomorrow. Why do we have to have this gangling boy on our hands.

"I didn't know what to do with him. And I knew Tom rather resented having his Thanksgiving vacation with a married couple. Though we were fond of each other . . . though Tom and I were very fond of each other. Well, we met him at the station and he jumped from the train and the trains were crowded with Carolina boys going to Richmond. And he caught hold of my shoulders, and he was just a little bit higher than I was at the time. He said, 'Mabel, you don't mind do you. I want to go to Richmond. I want to go with the boys.' Well, I knew they were going to be licked. I mean I don't know much about athletics but I knew it, just knew the general background of the thing. I knew they were going to be licked again. But they had their first victory the next day. A great victory in 1916 for the University of N.C.

"Professor Koch came from Dakota there to establish the first school of Carolina Playmakers, teaching playwriting. Tom was one of his first pupils along with Paul Green and Hubert Hefner and George Betty, and others and Elizabeth Lay who married Paul Green. Her sister Lucie and others. While Tom was a member of the Carolina Playmakers, he wrote 'The Return of Buck Gaven' and a couple of other plays and 'Gaven' was produced and he played the part of Buck Gaven himself. He played his own part in there and rather distinguished himself as a good playwright by this one act play.

"He graduated in 1920. He had been someone to be proud of. He had been editor of both the college papers. The second year he was perhaps the most popular man on the campus because they did appreciate his mentality. He wasn't so pretty to look at. He was a long, gangling Ichabod Crane personality. Big feet, thin, but a wonderful head. Always a wonderful head. His eyes and his hair and his face and he was serious minded and he loved people. And I don't think—he wanted things, but I don't think he wanted particularly this great popularity. He just wanted people to like him because he liked people.

"And he graduated from the University in 1920 and it had been pretty well decided by him and his teachers there that he was to go to Harvard to the 47 Workshop which was then being taught by George Stewart Baker. Dr. Baker and Tom became great friends at Harvard. And Dr. Baker believed in him. Tom was most enthusiastic in his playwriting. He dreamed and he wrote home that he'd get a play on Broadway and something that would live. And we of the family couldn't see much to that.

"We thought it took a genius or someone with great talent. We couldn't see anything in our family, our background or anything that deserved the name, Genius. And we couldn't feel . . . he was too close to us and we thought these writers and playwrights you know all the old ones like Tennyson and Poe and all of them, they were so removed they were on pedestals above us. We spoke of them as they were far away and we couldn't feel that someone so close to us had the power to write a play or to write a book. And no one had thought of his being a novelist at the time he was at Harvard.

"But Dr. Baker wrote home and asked Mama to produce the money one more year; that he would be greater than O'Neill, if they just gave him time. And then it was, I think, the last . . . he wrote several plays. I think there were seventeen short plays in all, housed at Harvard in the Houghton Library. I believe I'm right in that figure. 'My House' was one of them but 'Welcome To Our City' was given at Harvard the last year Tom was there. I don't know, there were just dozens and dozens of characters in the play. Too many for production down in New York. But Tom didn't realize that and didn't think of that part of it, of the cost of producing the play in the city.

"But they gave 'Welcome To Our City,' I think it ran until one o'clock at night. I've been told, I wasn't there, but it was quite a success.

"Mama's brother had been a Unitarian minister in Boston for years at Brookline. He'd been there for years. And his daughters and he and the family were wrapped up in Tom, very fond of him and saw him often and encouraged him and he thought his ability and we heard about that play from them.

"But the money had ceased at Asheville. Mama had been in this real estate boom at Miami and here at Asheville and there was no money. There was plenty of property but nothing to advance Tom any more and we, the other members of the family, didn't care to see her so harrassed. We thought he'd had about seven or eight years of college and these offers made to him to teach here or teach there, that he should take one. We thought he could do his work of playwriting along with his teaching.

"Tom went down to New York and submitted his play 'Welcome To Our City' to the Theater Guild and they kept it and kept it and he hung around New York and he wrote home that he was very hopeful because it had been so welcomed and so successful at Radcliff up at Boston. Why he thought surely that this Theater Guild would take it immediately. So one evening he went and the man who had the manuscript or who had the play, sat down at his desk, handed it to him, told him he couldn't use it. And Tom almost burst into tears. And the man was taken back by all this and he said, 'Oh, I'm sorry, I'm very sorry,' and he reached down, in his pocket and pulled out a ten dollar bill and handed it to Tom.

"I'm telling this story because Tom told this to me. And Tom said, 'Oh, no, no, no. I don't need the ten dollars. It isn't that. But, oh, I'm disappointed. What am I to do with myself. What am I to do.' And he said, 'Well, let's go out and spend it.' So he said that night the man told him that night . . . they spent the ten dollars out at a restaurant. And the man told him what the public wanted. The public wanted realism. They didn't want this fantastic writing. They wanted realism.

"Now whether that had anything to do with his writing *Look Homeward Angel* from his life story, from the web of his life, I don't know. But he went to Europe shortly after that. And coming back from Europe as a tourist, passage, I think, he was told by a young fellow that there was a woman on the top floor who wanted to meet him. That she belonged to the theater craft in New York and he wanted to take him to the first class section of the ship coming back, and to meet her. He went up and then it was he met Mrs. Bernstein, Aileen Bernstein, who became his friend and benefactor and helped him in every way she could after that.

"Tom came into New York. He had already taken the job of an instructor at New York University. And he came in from Europe and went to teaching that fall. But I believe he said he began his book, the book *Look Homeward Angel* before he met Mrs. Bernstein. He began it in London. And we knew nothing about a book . . . we didn't know for two or three years what he was teaching at New York University . . . that he had a book, that a book was in the making.

"We finally found out that he had something in the way of a manuscript which he wanted published, but we didn't think many people would read Tom's book. We were proud of him; to know he was a college teacher. We thought it was just fine if he would just go on and get to be the head of a department, the department of English, get a degree or someday probably have a small college of his own. But he was worried about not getting something published. Something *published*. And it was turned back and turned back, bounced back like a tennis ball, I understand, from various publishers.

"He went abroad in 1928 and he had met as I said earlier, a couple of years earlier, Mrs. Bernstein, and then it was that they wrote him and said that a publisher in New York was interested in his book, in his manuscript and on his return for him to stop in to see the publisher, which happened to be Charles Scribner.

"Tom said he took a boat right away. He sailed. That when he got this letter, he felt like the man

The tombstone shop of W.O. Wolfe, father of Tom. This building stood on the site where the Jackson Building now stands. Photo courtesy Pack Memoirial Library

who jumped on the horse and rode in all directions. He was elated, he was delighted, to know there was someone who was interested, who would even read the manuscript. He came back to America as soon as he could and the next day called on Scribners. He walked back and forth at 597 Fifth Avenue in New York City. He walked back and forth for a long time before he got the courage to go in and go upstairs and when he emerged from the place a couple of hours later, he was clenching something in his hand and he was so delighted that he found himself way up at 124th Street, up at Morningside Park, some place up there and he never knew how he got there, he said. And in his hand he was still clutching this thing and when he opened it he found it was a check for $500 dollars that Scribner had given him.

"The first money he was to ever receive for his writing. Then it was they decided on the name *Look Homeward Angel*. This of course, the title comes from Milton's *Lycidas*. And *he* changed the book with the help of Mr. Perkins the Editor. Mr. Perkins never collaborated, had nothing to do with one line of Tom's writing. Even his early letters to us at home, the kind of writing is the same as in *Look Homeward Angel*, the same as in his last book, *You Can't Go Home Again*.

"Mr. Perkins was a great friend. He believed in Tom. Tom needed someone to lean on, to talk to and when he, when . . . I mentioned a while ago, of his changing the book, I don't mean he changed the book, but he had to *cut out* a great deal of it which I believe was used in other books. But the story was just too long. They had to condense it to make a readable book, to make a saleable book.

"Well, he worked along for one year and he came home a month before the release of *Look Homeward Angel*. We were so proud of Tom. Not because a book was coming out, but because we feared the book. We wondered in our hometown here if there were ten people who would read it.

"We didn't know, we thought it would be some fantastic, silly little stuff. None of us dreamed that he had taken his characters from his life. That he had used his town. That he had had to do those things. That he couldn't pull things out of the air. I didn't know what he could write on. He hadn't explained it to us. I heard it was a man discovering himself or something. I had heard various remarks from Mrs. Roberts who seemed to know a little more about it than I did. And people would ask me on the street, 'What is Tom's book like?' I told them I didn't know. It would be out in October. He came home though, in September and I remember we had a big gathering at my home, a party, and I had invited all the people I knew who were literary or who were teachers or who could appreciate Tom. And he seemed pleased with the party. And the next afternoon, we carried him to the station. Our father was dead. We had mother in the car and Tom. Tom walked me down the tracks at Biltmore and he said to me, "Now, Mable, I want to tell you something. When I come again, I'll probably have to come incognito, I'll be wearing whiskers or the like.' And he saw that I was a little dumbfounded. And he said, 'You know, I have written in this book a few thing about people that I'm afraid some of them are not going to like.' He said, 'For instance, I wrote about a school teacher whipping a little boy,' or made some remark of that kind, I remembered it.

"But it went off me, it just rolled off. I never thought seriously of the book. I was the secretary of the Woman's Club, recording secretary, and it was the largest club in town. And most of these ladies were college bred and some Phi Beta Kappa's and they were the leaders of our town and of course they were more interested in the book it seemed, than I was. For us, it was just enough to have Tom. We loved him and to know that he was self-supporting and a college teacher and so forth and we never thought . . . . We thought the book wouldn't live very long anyway whatever it was. And so I went to my club meeting. And almost all, they came to me and told me how they were looking forward to, oh, looking forward with so much enthusiasm to the coming out or the release of this book. They wanted to read my brother's book. And I just yes'ed and thanked them and went away.

"But for the following meeting, two weeks later, the book had been released and I had received my copy and the whole town was buzzing. I was secretary of the Woman's Club, I think, because Tom Wolfe was my brother. I think they felt I wasn't capable of writing good papers but I could be a recording secretary. But I liked all the women and I think we had 120 in the membership. I had to go to the meeting. I had the books and the minutes of the last meeting and several letters to read and so on this Tuesday afternoon I went to our Woman's Club and the whole place was buzzing. I had stimulated myself with aromatic spirits of ammonia and braced until I thought I could go through a buzz saw, but when I got up to the door of the room they were standing around in groups . . . and if you ever heard about the locusts coming and the great noise they make in coming from a distance. But there they were, all buzzing and soon as they saw me, everything stopped. You could have heard a pin drop.

"I went into the room and my subconscious mind seemed to work at the same time I was carrying on. I knew they hated me. Some of my closer friends in that club, said 'Hello, Mabel' and sort of nudged up to the other one and away from me. I went up to the desk and had to start the meeting. I read their names and then I read some letters that were received and I read the minutes of the last meeting. We had a speaker that afternoon. A Judge Hyatt, Carl Hyatt. He was head of the juvenile courts here. He later became assistant United States Attorney General, I think, in Washington. He was there a number of years and his son here now is head of our police department, Carl Hyatt, Jr. But Judge Hyatt was there and everyone believed in his juvenile court work and he was to make a big talk on juvenile work and he knew Tom well and he made the speech, but during the time of his speech I hardly know what he said. I began to look the faces over in front of me and then it was that I knew how they disliked even the sound of our voice or anything. And I knew that Tom had disturbed them in his book and we hadn't heard compliments. Everyone was just completely stumped. And we of the family were shocked, too. It was so well connected up that I knew that people would begin to say they knew that was his family he was talking about. And I was so afraid they would feel that this party, this character, was so and so and this character was so and so. We of the family were not intellectual enough, if you call that intellectuality. We didn't know literature enough to know that what was written about our own lives which seemed in places sordid, and which was so innocent. We couldn't see great literature in that. But, of course, we loved Tom. That was the reason we could stand it.

"We didn't care for the literature. We didn't understand it anymore than the Asheville people. My mother and I began getting telephone calls. All day long the phone would ring. And most of it was sympathy for us. Sympathy that we had Tom Wolfe. And finally after about two weeks I went to town one day and one of my old friends from a large family here, an important family, she shook her fist right up in my face and she said, 'We know what to do with people like Tom Wolfe when he comes back. We know what to do. We're not going to have anything like all this in the book.' And I was completely startled. I thought of the years I had tried to sing, of the years that I had tried to be a singer and would have done almost anything to have been a singer. And I thought, after all, it was *fiction* I couldn't say I was Helen of the book and why should they take it to claim the characters? Why should they claim those characters?

"I rushed right home and wrote him a letter. I knew no one in the family had written him. I knew the shock of the town, the talk of the town and I said, 'Dear Tom. You certainly have put us on the map. We aren't nonentities anymore. And that would certainly please Papa if he could look down and hear and see a little that is going on. The whole world seems to be Wolfe conscious.' And I said, 'Don't you worry at all about what you've done. You are a writer now. I've had reviews from as far away as Chicago and they're all fine.' And I said, 'Even the reviews here in Asheville, *The Asheville Citizen*, particularly, was a fine review.' It was was written by Lola McCoy who is living here in the town. George McCoy was editor of one of our papers, *The Asheville Citizen* and Lola and George were always great friends of Tom's. And I said, 'Her review was fine in every way, but the town's talk crowded that out. We couldn't get much comfort from her review when the town was talking so.' But I said, 'You've put us on the map.' I said, 'I would have sold my ticket into Heaven if I could have gotten one inch of recognition such as you're getting in the press when I was trying to sing years ago.' I said, 'Now you're a recognized writer and that's what you want to be. You must go on with your next book.' I said, 'We're getting along fine. Mama is all right and none of us are going to die from it and we just want to know that you're all right.'

"Tom wrote me later and said they were the first kind words he had received from the town.

"But he fired me a telegram which is in our public library here. It read something like this. 'Thanks for your wonderful letter. Great characters in the book are Helen, Eliza, Gant, and Ben.' He said, 'No book shoud be read as gossip or judged by isolated passages. No characters should be judged by a mere line. Asheville, in time, will find I was trying to write a moving, honest book about great people.' He said that was the way the world outside of Asheville was taking it. 'Read over chapters on Ben's death and burial scenes. Does anyone dare say these aren't fine people?' He said, 'Tell Mama I'll write her in a day or so. Book selling fast. Looks like a success. Say nothing.' Then of course, he said, 'You're a fine person. Love, Tom.'

"Well, after all that fine telegram, I just put it in my pocketbook and every person I met who stopped me and were ready to say something or denounce him, I pulled out the telegram. If he wanted to write anything mean about Mrs. Brown or Jones, or a book just to make money, he'd have written one of those cheap little things. He'd have written one of those books, that would make money quickly. But he said, 'Don't they know that I'm trying to be an artist. I'm trying to be a writer. I meant to hurt no one. I thought of people generally. I was characterizing people (in traits) which were as true of people in London and Idaho as in Asheville. I just wanted to write books that would live.' And he said, 'I know now that it's like being dead. I must go on into the life that I've made for myself alone. I thought when the book came out and it struck my hometown there would perhaps be a few people there who would understand, who would read it and understand it. But now from all reports down there, I don't think there are many who haven't read it and all of them who have, read it as gossip. I meant to hurt no one.'

"And so he went on with his writing. The gossip went on and the talk went on in the town and I heard it from day to day.. But I lived here one year after the book came out and there were many people, I think back over it now, there were many people who understood from the beginning that the book was going to be a success and would live.

"I want to say for Asheville, I think they just followed the pattern of people when they were placed in a position to defend themselves. I think though, he didn't mention names or anything. I think people who were like certain characters felt that he meant them. But he said later he had to stick to the letter of his life. He could not just take things out of the air. He thought any first book was written with the knowledge of the author's life.

"I went to Washington the following year. My husband was the National Cash Register agent here but we were moved to Washington. And the great depression was on, it was 1930, and we went there to make a living. To go with the National Cash Register Company and to live. And I saw Tom a number of times. The first time after *Look Homeward Angel*, he had gone over on a Guggenheim Fellowship to Europe and he came down to Washington, I think it was in the spring of 1931. And during the years that I was in Washington which was from '30 to '37, Jan. '37, I think Tom made two dozen visits down to Washington. He'd go down to Virginia. He loved the South and he loved his native land. Although it was a self-imposed exile, he just couldn't make up his mind to go home again. To come back here to Asheville. I'd come in the summer time, sometimes twice during the year, to see my mother who remained here. But Tom would not come.

"He'd come to Washington and she, my mother, would come there twice a year to meet him. She would either meet him at my apartment (I was running apartments in Washington and had one for myself), she'd meet Tom there or visit me a day or so and go on to New York, and see him there. (My brother) Fred at that time, for part of that time, was Fairbanks Marshall salesman in Harrisburg, Pennsylvania, located there, Fredericksburg and Harrisburg. And he'd come down to Washington.

"I know several times at Christmas there, I had Mama, Tom, and ourselves. We were all trying to get a living and I guess we thought Washington was the place for it these days and I did see a great deal of Tom. Tom came down and he was teaching at New York and he'd go to Europe when he could get a little money together and he'd come back and hurry right down to Washington. We'd always take him over to Virginia. We'd ride him over to the Unknown Soldier's grave or over to Alexandria.

"I remember distinctly on a couple of occasions where he'd look into the future, look far away, and he'd look toward me and he said, 'Mable, this is the first time I've had my feet on Southern soil in so many years. Isn't it fine.' And he loved the trees of Washington. I remember the last time taking him and Fred, Fred was there, and Fred had never seen the Unknown Soldier's grave. It was cold in November, and we packed in the car and went over to Arlington and I made them get out of the car, because Fred hadn't seen the grave and I said, 'Go on, Tom, you go on around there. I won't get out of the car. I'll just stay here and wait for you. Go on around and see how they change the guard there and the grave and everything that goes on there.' And he came back and looked at

View from Elk Mountain Scenic Highway described in **Look Homeward Angel** *by author Thomas Wolfe where the young man in the novel shared a picnic lunch with his girlfriend, a boarder from his mother's rooming house, "Dixieland," as it was called in the book. Photo by Lou Harshaw*

Elk Mountain Scenic Highway north of Asheville. This was a popular area for the courting crowd who grew up in the town during the early 1900's when Thomas Wolfe was a young man. Photo by Lou Harshaw

me and he said, 'Now that's just seven times you've shown me the Unknown Soldier's Grave.'

"I came back to Asheville . . . Well, let me see what came next. *Of Time and the River* came out in 1935. *The Story of a Novel* came out about that time. He sent me *The Story of a Novel*, also the other book. He said "I've autographed it." And he said it was one of those special little books that was only for a few people, especially writers, those who were struggling to write. He didn't think the great general public would care to read it. And he hoped I would read it. It would only take a couple of hours. And then when *From Death to Morning* came out, he'd dedicated that to Ben. And Ben he loved very much. Ben being the only one in the family for a great many years. Ben's twin was dead and Tom, being the baby of the family threw their companionship, their feeling for each other more together than toward the rest of us. And he dedicated the book to Ben and he wrote a very beautiful inscription in that book to me. He wondered if Ben would have liked it had he lived. And would I ever forget that day 17 years ago. It happened to be 17 years on the very date that he sent me the book that Ben had passed away with influenza in the first flu epidemic.

"Tom came home.

"I came home in 1937 from Washington, to live (in Asheville) again and it was January. He came home in May that same year, to visit Mama and to hunt a cabin to write in, to be near Asheville, but to be alone.

"You never saw such a welcoming as Asheville gave him. They stood in groups around him on the streets and 12 to 20 (people) would be around him talking to him. Someone yelled one day and said, 'They're not wanting to kill you now Tom, because you put them in the book, but there are a number around here who would because you *didn't* put them in.'

"And he was received. Big dinners were given for him. And he was asked by the clubs and by the hotels to speak here and there. His picture was in the paper. Headlines were in the paper that Tom Wolfe was home. And we were all very happy. We were happy to know that the people were receiving him and he was delighted to know that there was no hatred in their hearts, that they wanted him home and were glad to have him and he wanted to come home. He chose the cabin out here near our Recreation Park. I would say four or five miles from the town. He got back on July the 5th, I believe that was the date, to take his cabin.

"He went back to New York from his first trip in May and came back to take the cabin over. I think he'd rented it from July 1st for just two months. But he came in around the 5th. He phoned Mama and said he was picking up a few things and he would see us before the day was over. I had prepared dinner, we had dinner anyhow, but he called me and said that he'd probably be out there and I thought it would be nice to have a little extra, but he phoned me almost at the last minute and asked if it would be all right if he went somewhere else. I told him to go any place he wanted to and just come to my place when it was convenient. I said, 'I know how it is, Tom, as far as the food is concerned we have to eat anyway, and come.' He came around 8:30 and I had a large divan in my room and he sat down on it. And I asked him if he were going over to Mama's. Mama, of course, had the boarding house and there were three or four members of the family living there. Our cousins, Effie and Ellie Wolfe and (my brother) Frank were living there and Tom and little Henrietta Westall, the child of Uncle Henry whom he characterized as Bascom Hawk, was there. Tom felt that it would be just too much of a strain to meet so many of the family, and to meet boarders, too. He said, 'Oh, Mabel, I'm so desperately tired. I don't have to go over there tonight, do I?' Well, I was only thinking of Mama. She had phoned two or three times and she hadn't seen him. He had visited her, of course, two months before and he would see her right away, the next day or so and I didn't stress it any further.

"And at 12 o'clock at night, we went into my little pantry breakfast room which looked right out at the great Grove Park Inn and the golf course and I asked him if he didn't want some cold supper. We had string beans, snap beans they called them and I had a dish of those and put them on the table right off the stove and I had warmed up some vegtable soup. These were things we had eaten in our childhood. We called it common food, vegetable soup, string beans, stewed corn. Tom consumed all of it. He was so fond of vegetables. He had told me often that those were things in

New York that he couldn't get. He could get always meat and bread. But he did get hungry for just mountain or country vegetables.

"And so, a little after 12, 12:30 or quarter of one he said 'I'll call a taxi.' And I said, 'You'll do nothing of the kind.' Ralph, my husband, had been reading the whole time out in the sun room, and I said, 'We're taking you out to the cabin.' And he said, 'Well, you don't want to go out there tonight, do you?' But he went. I told him we'd go if he promised not to stop downtown and go in a place and stay for hours, because he didn't have any idea of time. If he started talking and he wanted to talk, it could go into an hour and we were tired and it was very late.

"And he said, 'No, I'm awfully tired and I want to pick up some records and take them out.' We got out toward the cabin and the road that led off of this Recreation Park and it was dark as pitch. He had a flashlight. Then it was that he told me there was no lights in the cabin and he didn't have a lamp yet. And I had begged him to stay at our place but he said 'No, I don't want to. I don't want you to go in through the gates. It's a quarter of a mile, and you may get stuck, your car.' And he said, 'I'm going myself.' And I called him back and I said, 'Tom, please get into the car and go home with us. Don't go into that place tonight, by yourself like this.' And he said to me, almost shook the car, and he said, 'What do you want me to do, buy a gun and kill somebody?' He said, 'I'm not afraid.' And we just left him, left him there at the gate to walk the quarter of a mile.

"He called me then a day later and said that he was having a steak dinner for all members of the family. I think there were 13 of us here who were here in town who he had invited to that steak dinner. And we got out there on Sunday afternoon. He told us to come around four or five, whenever we wanted to. We got there around five and Tom was out sitting at a seat under a big tree looking up at a bird house. He was watching them. The cook had gotten drunk. He had a Negro cook, a man who had drunk some liquor and he was away and there wasn't a fire built in this old stove, and it was one of those how you have to make a fire with wood and everything. (So,) the fire was made to cook potatoes, bake potatoes, and to cook steak, but it seems now as I remember, we had a very good meal.

"Tom stayed here that last summer, 1937, and the whole town made a path to that cabin. They came across the watermelon patch in the back from a different direction. They came in bringing their own food, to go there to stay with him, to picnic with him and he got no rest.

"He left in September. He came into the hotel two days before leaving and registered there incognito and we took him out to the cabin to pick up a few things, came back to the hotel and had lunch in a place, the Raskeller there. He said, 'Now if I can just get across that lobby, and rest an hour or so, I'll be ready for that bus.' He was going to Roanoke, Virginia. I believe first to Bristol, Virginia, to visit a Mrs. Armstrong. Mrs. Armstrong now lives at the Broadhurst Theater Cottage up at Norton, Virginia. And he was going there, but a few days later, before he wrote us, after he got away that afternoon, a few days later we received a paper with his picture in it and it was a Roanoke paper.

"I should tell you that when he (first) came here to take this cabin, a few days later a large box arrived at Mama's house and the express charges I think were $7.50 which amazed her. She wondered what in the world Tom was sending this large pasteboard box of some kind, large, heavy thing that looked like a trunk and it was put in her old dining room which hadn't been used for years. Tom told her that was his mess bag and to guard it with her life.

"Of course, she knew he had writings in there, but she thought that he (also) had personal things in there. I mean wearing apparel, in the box. But he'd come in from day to day to see Mama and he'd go there, peek in that dining room from the side door to see if his box was still there and then when he went back, of course, he had ordered the box to be sent back to New York.

"He took up residence in the Chelsea and for weeks and weeks I think, he was deciding on an editor. He had severed his connection with Scribners because I believe, the reason for that was so many people wrote, so many people who are writing today wrote that they didn't know; they thought it was collaboration. They didn't know where Tom Wolfe left off and Perkins began. Maxwell Perkins, who was his close friend and whom he had dedicated *Of Time and the River* to and it was rather an extravagant dedication.

"Mr. Perkins was a great friend and all, but I, we all believed that Tom's writings would have found a publisher, would have been published. Mr. Perkins was very fine but no one had corrected

Thomas Clayton Wolfe while at Harvard University. Photo courtesy Pack Memorial Library

anything that had been written or said and these reviewers would make those remarks and Tom just couldn't stand it any longer. And he decided he would pull out on his own away from Scribners and Mr. Perkins and find his own publisher, a perfect stranger to him. (To try and) know just how good he was.

"So it was that he took up residence at the Chelsea Hotel. I don't know the details but I do know that Mr. Aswell who was with the Harper Brothers Publishing Company and one of the editors, went to Tom and visited him several times. One night Tom told him the story that he couldn't quite stand the sting of criticism of always mentioning his name with Maxwell Perkins and he wondered if he was good without Mr. Perkins' friendship and the fact that he could lean on him and so forth, and he was more a father to him.

"And he said, 'You know, Ed. I'm going to write a book.' About that time Mr. Aswell said, 'Tom, that's why I've been coming to see you. Harper Brothers will publish anything you write. We believe in you. I've come here for that very reason to find what you have to say about it.' He said, 'To show you how we feel about it, we know you have been worried with the economic situation, with your living. You've been hounded with bills, your living bills, and everything. We know a man has to often take a year, two years, ten years to write a book and we want you to feel secure in your living. Just to show you how my firm feels about you, how we feel about you, I brought this little thing along. I brought this along for you.' And with that, he handed him a check. And Tom walked away and looked at the check and it was for $10,000. And he came back, and he said, 'Ed,' he said, 'I never knew anyone believed this much in me.' He said, 'I'll give you the best that's in me if it costs me my life.' Now, I may have that a little wrong but I think that it is the idea. I think Mr. Aswell would agree with me there with what I said. Tom went to work. Of course, he had the box of manuscript which he had a way of writing, writing for hours and hours and hours. And he could go over to this box and lean down and pull out a piece of . . . a bunch of yellow stuff clipped together and it would fit right in and he could go on from there.

"He had written it from time to time so all of that could be had was his nest egg, was chapters of various books that he had planned for his saga of living. I remember once in Washington, when he was criticizing me for not coming to New York to see him oftener. I had all these apartments filled with government people and they were my own apartments. I mean I didn't own the property but I had rented and subrented and the little money I could make off of keeping them and having them cleaned and fixing them and renting them, was at that time what I lived on. My husband was ill and I said, 'I can't come up to New York, Tom.' I said, 'Washington has everything that I need in the way of city life. And you love it so down here. You love the treees and everything. You come here.' I had an idea that all his friends and all that literary world of editors and all were dressed so beautiful and lived so elegantly and I thought if I went up there in my simple attire and I didn't look the part of wealth that I would embarrass him more or less. And he said to me on one occasion, 'You mean that they're my friends, Mabel, they're not that kind. They're not that kind.' But we do get ideas that we are probably so unimportant ourselves that we might offend them by even being there and I just didn't make any great break to go to New York from Washington. I insisted but on this occasion, I said to him, 'Tom, everytime I go away from here I get a vacancy and I can't afford the vacancy because the profit I get on (those apartments) is our living and I can't afford . . .' And he said, 'I know Mabel, I know ever since the boom days, you've been worried about security.' And he said, 'I've been worried too.' He said, 'And I feel now I'm 33 or 34 years old.' It was about the time *Of Time and the River* came out. 'I feel that if I can live to be 50, I have it all planned,' he said. 'About 20 books.' And he looked over to my husband who was a quiet man, and he said, 'Ralph, I think I can get my say in 20 books. Don't you think I can?' And Ralph, said, 'Well, if you get your say in 20 books, Tom, you're the only Wolfe I've ever known who can get it out in 20 books.' He said, 'All the talk they do.'

"But I remember where he spoke of his security, and he was going to . . . and he said 'I know exactly how you feel and I'm going to get it and I'll get it in my 20 books.'

"Well, I came back to Asheville, and Tom came home and had his visit. He went back to New York in September and chose the Harper people and he worked very hard all winter. Worked into the nights and everything. I visited New York after his death and the Chelsea Hotel people told me that he would write until two and three in the morning and then just furiously write with nothing but coffee all day long, ordering coffee from the dining room and then he rushed down and he'd have to walk the city over before he could relax enough to drink a cup of coffee or eat a bite. That went on for a long time until in May he wrote us that he was going to the Northwest, that his book was about finished. But that he needed a vacation, he needed a rest. But he had been asked to speak at Purdue University. And he was stopping there first. Well, he wrote a very fine letter down here to Asheville just before he left, to me. He spoke on defeat and failure. He spoke a great deal about (how) nothing could defeat anyone who refused to accept defeat. And he wrote that I had always taken the hard road, but that the straight and narrow led no place. That you always learned more by going through the woods than taking the straight road and he wrote that he was going west. He was going to look at geysers and ride a streamliner and the like. That it was the only part of the country he hadn't seen and he was going there. It would only be a short trip, 3 weeks. But he was going to have a great time and he wished he could take me.

"I thought that was so foolish. I thought of my husband being ill and there's not much finance to take me to the Northwest and to do all that. But I was out there with him just a little later. Tom went to Purdue and he made this wonderful talk. I think he stuttered a great deal when he began his speech. I have a copy of that speech and I've been told by Herbert Morrow, who was a teacher of English there and also a Mr. Hastings, how Tom stuttered a little and then he began and he said to the boys, 'I've come out here to talk to you and I wish I could tell you how to be a writer, but I can't, because I'm trying to be one myself. I wish I could tell you, too, how to write a best seller, but I can't do that, for I'd like to write one myself. In all my writing years I've made less than $40,000.' Now this was 1938 and of course his book *Look Homeward Angel*, the first publication came out in late 1929. He said, 'I've made less than $40,000. However, I was in Hollywood last year and if I do what Hollywood wants me to do I can make that in a year I believe, there.' But he said, 'I'm not scoffing at Hollywood. I may come to that yet. But when I do I'll be like the old Belgian nun was when she was at the gates of the monastery when the Germans were entering the town and she just stood there and said, "When do the atrocities begin?" ' He said, 'I think people everywhere have a wrong idea about writers.' I think he said, 'My mother is as representative as any person I know.' He said, 'She is the finest and most hard working person I've ever known, but she sort of thinks that writing is a trick. Mama told an uncle of ours, who was a graduate of Harvard College, "Henry, why don't you do like Tom? Do nice, easy work and make a living instead of raising cranberries and getting out and working with the cranberries. Why don't you do nice, easy work like Tom? You're educated, too." ' "

"Tom said, 'I think they all believe it's like a trick, like being a sword swallower or something. 'I know,' he said, 'I told my mother, 'Now Mama the *Saturday Evening Post* paid me $1500 for that story.' And so she looked up to me, and she shook her head and she said to me, 'Well, child, if you get money like that for the kind of thing you do, you're mighty lucky, for all the rest of the family has had to work for a living.' Now, I don't know if Mama said that or not.

"But he said that Ms. Nowel, his agent, anyway, when he received the first money from the *Saturday Evening Post*, she said, 'Now Tom, the *Post* has ordered me to let them see everything that you write from now on. Not to give it to any other publishing company. They want to see everything.' So he said, 'I sat right down. I needed money, and I wrote I thought, the best thing I had ever written in my life. It had action, it had everything,' he said, 'the Post required. It was Post material.' And he said, 'It was my story "Chickamuga." I fired it right on to them.' And he said, 'I knew it would take two weeks to get an answer.' But, he said, 'In exactly eight days I got it. It came back. They couldn't use it. It wasn't *Post* material.' So Ms Nowel said, 'Don't worry too much about that, don't worry too much. There's *Colliers* and there's every magazine she mentioned. There's *Colliers's*, there's *Reader's Digest* . . . there's everything. We can get it published. There will be other magazines.' So we tried and each time it bounced back like a tennis ball. So finally I shelved it.' And he said in just exactly eight months it landed. He said 'Now no one should feel affronted about being published in the *World Review*. The *World Review* is an admirable little magazine He said they wrote me for something and I immediately picked up this "Chickamuga" and sent it to them.' He said, 'But the difference between being published in the *World Review* and the *Saturday Evening Post* is just $1400.'

"Well, after Tom left Purdue he went into Chicago and stayed a few days at the Palmer House with these two professors from Purdue and from there he went on to the Northwest. He went to Seattle,

Washington, and looked up some kin folks of our mothers, Ronnie and Elizabeth Harris and he met quite a few people. He met James Stevens, who was known as the Paul Bunyon of the Northwest and he knew Sophus Winters and his wife who were down from the University of Washington. He went over to Portland, Oregon, and there at the University Club he met Ed Burns, who is one of the editors of *The Oregonian* and Ray Conway who is head of the American Association of Autmobile people there and they were making a trip of the Northwest. Making a trip of the parks of the Northwest proving that tourists could go there, could make this trip in so many days or weeks. I think two or three weeks. And they were making a trial trip and they asked Tom if he wouldn't come along.

"Of course, that was just, using slang, 'up his alley' and he was delighted to go along. And he joned them at Portland, Oregon. Of course, a book did come out . . . *Western Journal*. He kept a diary of the whole trip. They would make five or six hundred miles a day. And then after that a matter of traveling, and their looking into everything and trying to observe everything, Tom would sit up and write of the day, and we had that manuscript on our way back. And he would leave pages in between the days showing that he intended to continue out and write more, write a longer story of the whole thing, make a book out of it.

"But he went on and came back to, I think it was Olympia, Washington, where the trip ended on July the 6th. I believe I'm right, it was July 6th and he went into Seattle from Olympia. When he got back to the hotel, why he stayed around there for a few days and decided he'd go over to Vancouver and take that trip and he went to Victoria and then into Vancouver and when he got there to the hotel, I don't know the name, he was very ill.

"He got his room and went up to his room and stayed a full 24 hours and came down the next day. He'd decided that he would take the train back to Seattle where he knew people and he said to an old club man, I think it was around 3 o'clock in the afternoon, 'How much of Vancouver can you show me in three hours before my train leaves?' And they agreed on spots. He said, 'I don't think I can even get out of the cab. You'll just have to drive me to places and let me see as much as I can.' And they agreed on this and toward seven o'clock when the train left for Seattle, I think it makes the trip in four or five hours from Vancouver into Seattle, why Tom said, he went down and it was more, the way these customs officers there looked at him and made remarks about him, as he passed them. He was holding his side and he was in great pain and I presume running a high fever then but he went down and got on the train.

"There was an old Negro porter, and this porter came to him seeing his distress, and he said, 'John, can you fix me up, get me a comfortable place to sit and put a blanket around me. I'm chilling and I'm sick.' And he said, 'Come this way' and took him to the observation car and put him in the leather seat and wrapped a blanket around him and Tom got into Seattle around midnight, 11 o'clock. He went to the new Washington Hotel where he had stopped before and he said the little clerk behind the desk gave him a big wink and he said, 'I don't know if I can fix you up or not. The house is filled with Sunday School teachers.' And then turned around and said 'I have this room' and they took him up to the room.

"I can't give you the date, but he went to the home of the Winters (friends of Tom) and got there late. He was invited to join this group for the dutch supper and he came in late and they were all putting their books in front of him for an autograph and talking to him and I heard this from Jim Stevens and his wife. This was Friday night. Tom seemed feverish and rather high and full of this whatever this virus was or whatever was wrong with him. And they didn't hear anymore from him until Monday afternoon. Monday afternoon he phoned the White Lumber Company and got Jim Stevens and he said, 'Jim, remember the other night when someone mentioned a certain medicine for a cold or cough. Do you know what that is?' And said, 'Where are you, Tom. We've been worrrying about you. Where are you?' Tom said, 'I'm in the hotel here.' He said, 'From Friday?" Tom said, 'Yes, from Friday. The bellboys have been taking care of me.' He said, 'Are you able to get dressed and get in a cab? I'll meet you over here at Fourth and Pike.' He met him and took him up into Dr. Ruge's office. Dr. Ruge was their doctor. Dr. Ruge had a sanatorium at Kenmore Crossing just outside of Seattle, Washington and Tom, I've been told, when the first sickness came on him, his first temperature, he had a really dreadful time. He was so feverish that he was really high. We wanted a plane to get back to New York. He didn't know what those people would think of his getting sick.

"His temperature was 106, went as high as 106. Dr. Ruge rode him out to Kenmore Crossing, his own sanatorium which was only a private sanatorium for nervous people. But he was I think the first person in that part of the country who had closed the lung, had collapsed the lung. He was considered a very fine doctor. He didn't have the facilities of taking, getting blood transfusions, of taking blood tests, all the hospitals have.

"Fred went out right away. Fred, our brother, who heard the news here through Harpers. Harpers heard the news from Dr. Ruge and then they wired Fred. Fred was in Seattle almost four weeks before he phoned me and Mama.

The Wolfe family in front of their home on Woodfin Street. The members are, left to right, Effie, W.O., Mabel, Fred, Grover, Ben, Julia and Frank. All the children were born in this house. Photo courtesy Pack Memorial Library

"Tom's fever had come down but he was still ill and they were still treating him. He still couldn't rise from the dreadful illness. But yet they said he was coming along beautifully. Nothing could happen.

"Fred phoned me one night and I'd had a very sick husband all summer, and he said, 'Tom wants you out here Mabel, He wants you to come. Mama's too old for such a trip but he wants someone on the outside to look after him.' He said, 'I've been here four weeks and of course I have my business to get back to. But I'm not leaving him alone unless you come and relieve me.' So of course, I left the next night. I got to Seattle and one of the first things Tom said, he seemed to look at me in rather a furious way first and he said, 'Have you come out here to tell me how sick I am?' And I had been with a very sick man, my husband had been ill. And I said, 'Tom, I think you look fine, to have been ill five weeks.' I guess it was then five weeks. 'I think you look fine.' You have that rested look.' But I realized he had also a very depleted look. Perspiration seemed to still pour, although he didn't have a temperature, there was something wrong. Something. But we brought Dr. Schoenwald who was an excellent doctor, a consultant, a big man whose fee was $30 a trip out there to see him.

"Oh, by the way, I haven't told you. Fred went, he went out and they put him in Providence Hospital. And they put this consultant Dr. Schoenwald and the attending physician Dr. Watts, in charge of him. They were the hospital doctors, at Providence Hospital. Providence could take blood tests and give transfusions and do those things that a private sanatorium didn't have the facilities for.

"And Fred and the doctors thought it was best and Tom wanted to leave the sanatorium too, because it was for nervous wrecks and so forth and he felt he would be better off in a regular hospital. So they moved him to Seattle, of course by ambulance. And he was in this hospital for four or five weeks.

"Fred asked me if I could take the train the next night when he telephoned and I took the train out of here, Asheville, N.C. for Seattle. I got into Seattle, Washington, I think August the 19th, and I was met by my brother Fred. And we went out to the hospital and after seeing Tom and his being a little distressed for a moment as to my opinion of his condition. I went out to talk to this consultant, Dr. Philip Schoenwald. Dr. Schoenwald was considered a very fine consultant, a very expensive man. He was from Vienna and they called upon him just for consultation.

"And I went out and I said, 'My mother is worried so in Asheville and wants to come if he is in danger.' He said, 'Oh, no. Let your mother stay back there.' He said, 'We will be sending her boy back to her in just a little while.' He said, 'Tom is getting along fine.' He said, 'He just must have time to get his rest.' He said, 'He's been doing fine. You'll just wire your mother to stay where she is.' And so that relieved the whole worry about it. I went back in the room.

"In two days Fred left for Asheville much against his wishes. Left Seattle but he didn't see any reason, the doctors didn't see any reason, for both of us being out there so far away from home. His business going to seed, and I felt I might need a little trip and it was all right with me and I was glad to stay with Tom. But I knew he would get rid of me very quickly because I had a sick husband to get back to and I went to the hospital daily and every day he seemed to get better. And every day they told me that he would soon be out and the last week, which was along about Sept. 1, his attending physician Dr. Watts, had to make a state tour, to go to a state convention and he was gone.

"It's a Catholic Hospital, Providence is, and the nurses and all had said that Tom would have to be released from the hospital by the attending physician who happened to be out of town.

"I had gotten an apartment at the Spring Apartment Hotel to begin on a certain date, any date that we could get there, but certainly by this date, when Dr. Watts was expected back in town. Tom seemed to be hungry although the hospital food wasn't bad and I'd go across to a drug store and have a little lunch. I'd go out in the morning around ten and I'd stay until around nine at night around the hospital. It was two miles from the center of town where my little hotel, the Hungerford was and I'd go out there and Tom would eat what was on the tray and I'd go across to the drug store particularly and bring him ice cream. He liked that and I read two or three books out loud to him. Mr. Perkins had sent some light literature out there and he was delighted with these stories and the days went quickly and he seemed to be getting along fine.

"Finally Dr. Schoenwald came in on Friday about Sept. the 1st or 2nd. He came in to make an examination and he immediately threw his hands out and he said, 'Tommy, my boy, we were quite worried about you when you came to us, Watts and I were. You know that spot on your lung was this big,' and he made a sign of a silver dollar about that large. He said, 'We were worried. But now that has shrunk down until it's about the size, oh it's the size of a nickel or a quarter, so small there and it's healing rapidly, in fact,' he said, 'we thought of collapsing the lungs.' And oh, Tom went up in the air about that. The idea . . . he thought collapsing a lung was the worse thing ever. He said, 'But we found out you're just all right, Tom. All you have to do now is go with your sister down to the Spring Apartment Hotel,' where I'd got an apartment and he said, 'Just lay around a little and rest a little.' And he said, 'My wife and I are coming to see you.' He said, 'She reads your books and she is very fond of your writing. And Mrs. Schoenwald and I are coming to see you and your sister.'

"And then they began talking of Vienna, his hometown, and all the music halls, and the musical people and he told of losing his home to Hitler and all that and how his home had cost $17,000. I remember that. And they talked about some of the restaurants. Tom turned to me whom he thought was more or less ignorant about things to tell me about how I would love it because of the music. Oh, he mentioned some great percent it seems to me it was 70 percent of the people were more or less musical in that part of the country. Dr. Watts left with smiles and everything was just fine. This was Saturday.

"That afternoon Dr. Watts was to come in around 7 o'clock. There was a nurse there from Asheville and she'd been very loyal to us in coming to see him and bringing him nice things, something to eat and flowers and so forth. (I said to Tom) 'I think she is coming this afternnon, but I'll be back tonight and go down and get all this food that we talked about to move into this Spring Apartment Hotel. They had a beautifully electrcally equipped kitchen right next to this beautiful apartment that look right out on Puget Sound. And I went to town and went down into the markets of Seattle and battled with them and I got everything I could think of that he talked about. I got loin lamb chops, porterhouse steaks. He even wanted pickled peaches. He was hungry for vegetables, golden bantam corn, green beans and we were going to have cornbread. I found buttermilk. I was so proud I got out of the taxi and carried it back to the hotel and put it in this icebox at this Spring Apartment Hotel and I fell across the bed and I went sound asleep. It was then six or seven o'clock and I didn't wake up until nine and I called up the hospital and found that he was doing well. I said I tried to get Dr. Watts and I couldn't get him at his home but I'll go there in the morning early, and Tom can leave the hospital tomorrow morning on Sunday. And so the next morning I went out to the hospital and there was still no Dr. Watts and we packed everything.

"Tom got up. I found his trousers were much to large for him and we found a pair of suspenders in his suitcase. I think he had worn them from time to time to hold everything together. And so we put those on and with the assistance of these two large safety pins. And we thought we were leaving right away in the afternoon and we thought they were through with him and everyone thought he was all right. And I never saw him happier.

"I had packed . . . he wanted every magazine taken with us and he wanted all his books he had been given and everything. People had sent him little presents of various kinds, jellies and pies. All that had to be packed. He wanted everything because he saved everything. And finally around 12 o'clock or a little later, Dr. Watts came in the room and he said, 'Hello, Tom, how are you.' Tom was up and dressed. 'I've been looking over your chart down here and that headache hangs on doesn't it.' He said, 'Yes,' he said, it does, that medicine doesn't quite relieve it.' He said, 'I find when I sit up on the bed and throw my feet up on this ottoman, here that it doesn't ache. But when I lie down it aches, the pressure or something.' Dr. Watts said, 'Well, let me see.' He said, 'Let me see if they have an (Dr. Watts named a medical machine. This is unintelligible in transcription) here in the hospital.' Immediately Tom put his hand up to his head and evidently he knew what the instrument was and he said, 'Oh, my God, I hope you don't find a tumor.' I said, 'Oh, tumor my eye.' I said, 'Why are you always upset about it, of course you have no tumor.' Well, we waited for a long time and still no Dr. Watts. And I walked out of the room down toward the sun parlor. I thought if he came back I wanted to give Tom a chance to talk to him alone.

"But when I came back through the hall, Dr. Watts was coming out of the room and he said, 'Oh, Mrs. Wheaton, I want to speak to you a minute.' And he immediately said, 'I've just looked in Tom's eye. It looks to me as if on that right side there, there is a chocked disc.' He said, 'Now don't be alarmed at a chocked disc.' But I didn't know what a chocked disc was. He said, 'I think the smart thing he ought to do is to stay here now until tomorrow morning and let me bring a good eye man out here. I don't think I'll bring a specialist or surgeon. I'll bring Bonnet, my associate.' But he said, 'You get the nurse, that nurse who is a friend of yours and Tom who comes here to see you from Asheville. Tell her to be here too.'' And he knew Miss Crawford, he had taught her. She was in a class she was taking a psychiatry course over at the University of Washington and he knew her and so he went.

"And I went over to the telephone to phone Mama's cousin who was to take us downtown to the Spring Apartment Hotel in his automobile. He lived across town . . . to keep him from coming until the next day and I told him what had happened and about this time I looked toward the elevator and Miss Crawford, the nurse was getting off the elevator. And I said, 'Oh, I'm in luck, Dr. Watts has just been here and we can't go until tomorrow.' And then I told her what he'd said about a chocked disc and all and she threw her hands up and she said, 'Oh, Mabel, Let's get him out of this hospital as soon as we can. They're giving him enough dope here,' she said, 'more than a whole institution should take.' And we went back into the room and Tom's dinner had come in. It was the best meal of the week it was Sunday dinner and he usually got a pretty good tray of stuff that he liked. The nurse in charge of the floor was in there with a long pill that was somewhat green, blue or green, and he picked it up in his fingers and looked at me and said, 'I'm taking horse medicine now. Look at the size of this.' But he swallowed it and he seemed to get completely far away. I don't know if he spoke to Miss Crawford or not and she had come to see him and had been most kind all the way along.

"I don't know what happened but I was a little bit upset with him and I said, 'Now listen here, Tom. There's no use in your getting morose because you have to stay over here another day. You know they had me gasping too. Now, I'm coming out here tonight and I'm going to stay until you go to sleep but we're going out of here in the morning. They've been talking of your leaving the hospital for a week but we are leaving in the morning.' And he said, 'You'll get behind them, won't you Mabel.' And I said, 'Yes, you're going in the morning.' And all the while he was throwing the food in not particularly noticing what he was eating and I said, 'I'm going downtown to get dinner. I haven't had anything to eat.' And it was getting on after 1 o'clock, 1:30 and I said, 'The dining room closes at two at my little hotel, the Hungerford, and I want to write a few cards and write Fred a letter.' Fred would always take my letters . . . I'd send him the effort of writing, and I'd send air mail, or course and he was at Spartanburg and he would call Mama on the telephone. But if I wrote Mama the letter, she was more economical than Fred and she would wait to write it down and send it to him and so I knew Fred regardless of expense, would read the letter over the telephone to her. And I knew one letter would do in that case. I'm not as good a writer as Tom. And so I said, 'I want to write Fred a letter and write a few cards.' And he said, 'If you write to anyone whom I know, you might remember me to them.' And I left the room, went on down to the Hungerford and got there in time. I remember exactly, it was 10 minutes til two when I entered the dining room and then after dinner I went upstairs on the mezzanine and got some cards, and began writing the letters and cards and around 4:30 the phone rang on the desk. I didn't answer it, it was just a public stenographer's desk and she was gone. It was Sunday and finally a bellboy came running in and said, 'Oh, Mrs. Wheaton, that's for you.' He knew you were up here and so I went to the phone and it was Miss Crawford calling. She said, 'Did Tom seem all right to you this morning when you were here?' And I said, 'Perfectly, perfectly.' I didn't know what she wanted. 'He seemed so happy and he helped me bundle his books up and his magazines.' She said, 'I don't think he's known a thing all afternnon. I don't believe he's known it was I in the room.' And she said, 'Will you come to the hospital. I've got to go back over to Harvard here,' the hospital where she was taking her course. 'But I wish you would come to the hospital' she said. And I said, 'I'll get there right away.' I caught a streetcar and this was my habit. I didn't think it was anything particularly to hurry about, but I went right away, I didn't go back to the room. I got out and Tom was standing at his door when I went up to . . . got out at that floor and he was standing there and he looked and he saw me coming and he was in his blue pajamas and looking quite fresh and fine. And he said, 'Hello there Mabel, how'd you get out here. Did you come by plane?' There I'd been all the time. He said, 'Did Henry Westall bring you?' We have a cousin here named Henry Westall, who I've always been very fond of and Tom connected my name with his all through this thing. He knew it, too, that was in his mind. Henry had cars. And I said, 'Tom, you know I came on that streetcar right out the window.' And he said, 'I don't like you to do that. I don't like you to do that. You know fifty people in this town with autumobiles.' But I didn't know anyone except the Stevens and the Winters, who had called. I knew no one because I knew no one.

"And I said, 'Darling, come on and get back in the bed.' I had rubbed on his head during the time I was there just quarts of mentholated woodshavings. He had resented the smell of alcohol. He got so he couldn't stand the odor of it to be rubbed on his body. And he had these headaches but when I could soak his head, his black hair, and his head with this, the cooling effect seemed to (make) . . . the headache cease. And I had done that. I said, 'Come on get back in the bed, you've been up too long.' And I said, 'Who's been here and everything' and as I began rubbing his head, he said, 'Oh, I don't know, I don't know. They've been passing before me, everybody has been here today.' And pretty soon he went off in a little slumber and I rushed down the hall and asked the sister in charge. And she said, 'Oh, I don't know. No one's been here but that nurse.' And anyway, I stayed there that night until they made me leave and Mrs. Muller who was very nice, the night nurse whose husband was an intern at another hospital and she was very nice, she said, 'I'll look at him, I'll watch him all night.'

"Tom didn't have any private nurse. He wasn't considered sick enough for that. I didn't know what had happened. I thought his nerves had collapsed. I thought he was too filled with dope. I didn't know what was wrong. But I went back and had a restless night and got to the hospital early the next morning and the nurse was already there, Miss Crawford, and Tom was soon taken up to the operating room, up to look at his eyes or something. And I went over and got a cup of coffee, came back and pretty soon he came back to the room in a wheel chair and he said to me, "I drank all that white stuff and I'm awfully sleepy.' I don't think he drank anything. I think that he said, 'I'll just lie down Mabel and I'll just sleep a little.' And I said, 'All right, you do that, honey.' And the orderly who had brought him back and I looked out and down the hall and there the doctors had come down and there they all were huddled near this cupboard. And I rushed down the hall and they said to me, 'Now, Mrs. Wheaton, we just looked in Tom's eyes.' And he said, 'There is pressure there and it shows . . . pressure there in the brain. Now of course we don't know exactly what that may be, but tumor or something.' He said, 'But we want you all to go down to the Spring Apartment Hotel and rest a day or two and then go to Johns Hopkins to Dr. Walter Dandy. He is the best in the country and if there is anyone who can save him it is he.'

"Well, I was just completely stunned. I was astonished. After all I had heard of his being definitely on the road to recovery, definitely all right. After they left, I sent a telegram. I got Watts to write the telegram to Mama and Fred at Asheville. I called in Dr. George Swift, he asked if I had left the hospital and I told him no, that we were going right in an hour or so.

"We went down there to the Spring Apartment Hotel and Dr. George Swift came up. Tom was so tired when we got to the Spring Apartment Hotel he just fell across the bed. I don't think he ever knew the luxurious surroundings that we were in. The apartment was perfectly beautiful. Friends who knew he was going there and that he had been so desperately ill, had sent him magnificent flowers. There were gladiolas that looked to me to be 6 to 8 feet long in tall white vases. Everything was that beautiful white furniure, gold and white crested stuff. And they had put the largest bed they could find in this huge living room that looked out at this little porch up to Puget Sound. And he just went into sleep with his eyes half open. But Miss Crawford and I got in the kitchen and we were waiting for Dr. Swift to come between seven and eight and we thought we'd get dinner over and we cooked everything that we could think of and the place was just stacked with food. Tom got up to eat. We rolled him over by the window or pulled him. And I said, 'Tom, do you know where we are, dear?' And he said, 'In a fine hotel, fine hotel. I think you chose well this time Mabel.' When I got the apartment, he had known where it was and I wanted to go to one down the way that was just half the price. I had said to him, 'Tom, you know the other apartment is just the same size and almost as well decorated.' It seemed such a shame because money had been very scarce with us and I didn't think I ought to go loose with his. I knew he was to pay the bill and he said, 'Now listen, Mabel, we're going to have the best of everything now. We're not going haywire or anything with money, but we're going to have the best of everything.' He said, 'You know parsimony has killed more people than anything else.' He said, 'Let's not be parsimonious now. Let's have the best of everything. I can afford . . . I can afford it now.' And so that's why I'd taken this apartment. And then when we got there this big beautiful double bedroom for Miss Crawford and me and this huge

140

One of the last "celebrations" held in honor of Fred Wolfe, brother of Tom, before Fred's death. It was sponsored by the Thomas Wolfe Memorial at the boardinghouse in Asheville. Fred was awarded a plaque and three women, who had contributed services over many years to the Memorial, were also honored. Photo by Lou Harshaw

mammoth almost a reception room. We placed a bed for him and this lovely electric kitchen and private bath. And at 8 o'clock Dr. Swift came. Dr. George Swift, the brain specialist.

"He'd heard of Tom. He'd been written to in the beginning by Harpers. But being a brain man, and Tom, not needing a brain surgeon, he didn't go in. He'd gone off on his summer vacation and been gone most of the summer.

"We were so bolstered up to have Dr. Swift to arrive at 8 o'clock. We felt sure, you know that his diagnosis would be exactly the opposite of what the hospital had told us. We knew he was a brain man and I was so sure it was the dope, the headache dope and the various pills he'd taken that had unbalanced him in some way. And yet in some ways Tom was perfectly rational. He could tell the person when they would come into the room, he could call them by name. But then he'd go off in a dream like of something that had happened in the past.

"And when Dr. George Swift entered the room and met us he spoke of the beautiful flowers, the beautiful apartment, the part of the country we came from. He spoke to Tom and he said, 'Tom, I've heard a great deal about you. And he said, 'Well, I've heard a great deal about you, Dr. Swift.' The doctor said, 'You know Harpers thinks the world and all of you, you're a big man.' And Tom said, 'Well, I think you're a big man, Dr. Swift.' And that conversation went on. Tom was piled up in the bed with pillows back of him and waiting. And he said, 'You know, I've come to see you, your sister called me and with your permission I'd like to examine you, take,' I think he said, 'your reflexes or something.' And anyway Tom permitted that and said, 'Well, well, that's fine Dr. Swift.'

He sort of struck his knee, his right knee and he said, "That is the right side of my right leg and that's the left side and that's that.' And finally, Dr. Swift said, 'Let me look in your eyes, Tom. I just want to look in your eyes.' So he allowed that and he said, 'Um, um.'

"He walked over to the window, a good length, and looked up to the Sound and then spoke again of our view and he said, 'Tom, I want to tell you something. Why do you want to go down to California?" Tom had wanted to go down to Palo Alto to be with his friend Dr. Russell Lee, to be there for his convalescence. We had sort of planned that and I had told Dr. Swift and he said, 'Why do you want to go anyplace except to a place where they can find out what's wrong with you?' He said, 'You're desperately ill. Don't let anyone tell you differently.' By that time I had rose to my feet and caught hold and he said, 'Now, Mrs. Wheaton, you just be quiet. Tom can take this. He's a big man.' He said, 'You're desperately ill, Tom. You owe it to your family, to your public and to everyone who cares for you to get well.' He said, 'We haven't the facilities here. You should have left tonight, you and your sister.' And he said, 'But, I'll get reservations and you must go from here tomorrow and go to Johns Hopkins Hospital where there are two dozen men who can find out what the trouble is, and get you well.'

"Well, by that time I'd gone from the room. I left the room. I was just battling with myself to keep from blowing up and I went out into the hall and Dr. Swift came out and he caught hold of my chin and he said, 'Head up. You can take it.' He said, 'He is desperately ill.' And so we called Mama up and Fred at Asheville. It was after nine o'clock there at Seattle but it was after twelve or one here, and he talked to her and Fred and I left the next night. It was a bad day. I did a million things that day, but Tom dozed off and on all day. He could drink orange juice. And he talked, as

The Wolfe family graves at Riverside Cemetery. Photo by Lou Harshaw

I said, rationally and irrationally. He seemed happy enough. And the nurse was trying to get her things to get ready to go. All the doctors were there. People gathered downstairs. They knew he was so sick, But along in the evening, our train left at 10:30, the Olympian. Dr. Swift called me up and he said, 'Now you be smart and don't take him down in the automobile.' We had brought him to the hospital in an automobile from the hotel the night before. And he said, 'Don't let your cousin or anyone else talk you into taking him down in an automobile.' Our cousin was a Christian Scientist, was a convert Christian Scientist and he thought Tom was all right.

"He said, 'You order an ambulance from the Shepherd Ambulance Company and you get that boy out of there before the train time. Get him on the train, you can get on after 9 o'clock.' So I just looked at him and Miss Crawford, the nurse and Tom and just before he left the room I gave him the money to pay the ambulance people. I had been handling the money and gave it to Tom. He called me over and he pulled me down and I said, 'What is it, Honey, what is it?" He said, 'Have you a couple of extra dollars. I want to give it to them.' He knew these two fellows. They had brought him to Providence Hospital and there they were. They knew him and they were laughing and talking with him.

"So he went on to the train and I went down later with about nine different pieces of baggage and with my cousins, Lonnie and Elizabeth Harris. And we left all these people in the lobby down-stairs. It seems as I think now, there must have been two dozen waiting there to say goodbye to him and me. I got to the train and saw Dr. Watts before I got on the train. He said, 'You'll make it all right.' I said, 'He's all right, isn't he, he's going to get well isn't he? There's nothing much wrong is there?" And the only remark he made was, 'You'll make it all right. You'll get there all right.' Dr. Dan was a fine doctor, so it was really a blessing. I just praised God when the wheels began to turn taking me East.

"We had two compartments and he was in the lower berth of his compartment and we didn't take the upper one down and Miss Crawford and I were in the other compartment. We pulled the door open between and I was in the upper one. I was so tired that she had insisted on my going to bed and getting a little sleep and she would stay up and watch him. But she went off to sleep and along about two o'clock in the morning the door opened and this great flash of light from the hallway and here was the trainman, the conductor, or one of the trainmen, holding Tom by the arm. I jumped up from my upper berth and looked down and he said, 'Hello, Mabel, how are you up there?"

"I found he had gone through seven steel cars to the observation car back that way hunting the telegraph office. He told them he had to wire his friends. He didn't know what they would think. He'd gone and so the trainmen told us that if either of us, both of us wanted to go together to the diner or anyplace to please notify one of them and they'd sit with him. But we never left him.

"I got up at that moment. I didn't try to sleep the rest of the journey across the country. I sat on the floor at night on a cushion and put cold towels on his head and we talked the whole way across the country at night. Miss Crawford would take care of him in the daytime, make up our part of the room, a compartment and she'd sit there and then I'd sit in there, but most of the day I stayed out as much as I could. He ordered great trays of food. He loved roast beef and steaks and baked potatoes and things of that kind and desserts and tea. He drank gallons of tea, coming across the country. We got into Butte, Montana and he looked up there and saw this . . . . He said, 'This is the richest hill in the world' I believe he said. He was talking about the mines at Butte, Montana. This was the richest hill in the world. He knew that.

"Then at other times, he would think that we were going through China. That they raised such amounts of rice. That the people depended upon the rice and that we were there. Finally, we got into Chicago where we had to change trains. Of course, after a four day, three night run across the coun-try. And we got into Chicago and Mama met us there. I had been getting telegrams all across the country from the family and Mama met us at Chicago.

"At the Union Station I got a reservation on the Pennsylvania. We went out around 11 or 12 o'clock noon to Baltimore. We got into Baltimore on Saturday morning. My dates are sort of misty now, but Saturday morning . . . Tom died on the 15th and this was about the 10th . . . Saturday morning and the Hopkins people were there. The ambulance was there and an intern or two to take him. But he was all ready to go, but he didn't know quite where he was going. And when he was lying on that stretcher in the station and I again had to take a taxi with all the baggage up to a

143

rooming house opposite the Johns Hopkins Hospital where I'd often stayed when my father was ill and would be back and forth to Baltimore for radium treatment.

"Tom was up and he said, 'Where are you taking me to now?' Mama was standing there and I said, 'Well, Tom we're taking you up to Johns Hopkins Hospital.' I knew he rather loathed the place. He dreaded the place because of Papa having gone there so much. And I said, 'I want to tell you one thing, Tom, You're going up there where all these people can find out what's causing all this and when you get all right, you're going across the country and you won't be bothered with a single member of your family.' I said, 'We won't be following after you, but we just can't stand to see you sick like this. You can go right back by plane, too. You can go to Palo Alto to see Dr. and Mrs. Lee.' And he said, 'Well, your idea, Mabel, about Johns Hopkins might be all right but I have ideas of my own.' And I said, 'Well, darling, what are your ideas?' He said, 'I want to rest. I'm awfully tired.' Well, I left him and I followed the ambulance in a taxi. The taxi waiting in front of my place until the ambulance had gotten all the way up to the door to take him in. I went over later and he had eaten a good breakfast. Mama was with him and, of course, the nurse, too.

"I wish I'd really been in good shape. But that day Tom had his lunch and while he was eating lunch, the phone rang for me. I was with him and Mama had gone across the street to our room and Fred . . . I hadn't phoned Fred then that he must come from his place and also to wire the others to come if they wanted to. I was in the room and they called me to the telephone. When I got there, he said, 'This is Mr. Aswell talking. Is this Tom's sister Mrs. Wheaton?' He said, 'Well, how is he?' I said, 'He's just fine. We're waiting for Dr. Dandy. He comes in about 2 o'clock.' He said, 'Well, I'm at the station. Tell Tom I'll be there in just a few minutes. Hold off until I get there.'

"Oh, I just thought that was wonderful that Mr. Aswell was there with us and before this examination. I went back to the room and I said, 'I have good news for you Tom, Mr. Aswell is here.' And he said, 'Oh, thank goodness.' And Mr. Aswell came in a few moments and went in the room and Tom raised right up out of the bed and said, 'Howdy Ed, how are you.' He seemed to be perfectly himself. He said, 'I'm so glad to see you, Ed.' I knew he worried about his unfinished work. I knew he worried about the money he'd taken from Harpers having not given them anything, his work being more or less finished but not yet selected for the book.

"And Mr. Aswell said to him, 'Tom, we've read over everything. It's all fine. It's splendid. All of it is splendid. Now I want you to know that Harpers isn't worried at all about those books, their publication. We want you to get well. We are willing to just wait and we want you to get perfectly well. What you've written is splendid.' And he said, 'Oh, thank you, Ed, oh thank you.' And about that time the door opened and in came Dr. Dandy with three or four other doctors of the hospital. I think Dr. Hammonds was one, for the lungs, and of course we went out.

"And it wasn't any time just two or three minutes. I was getting acquainted with Mr. Aswell. I hadn't met him up until then and I was out in the hall and I said to him, 'Oh please, he won't tell me anything. I'm too upset, too nervous, and too tired to find out what the trouble is, what it's all about, what causes Tom to be like this. To be irrational and what is wrong anyway.' And he said, 'I'll do my best, and don't you come in. You leave it to me.' So, presently, Mr. Aswell and Dr. Dandy went together into a room and out came Mr. Aswell calling for me. And I called for Mama, who was holding herself together over in the living room of the Marlborough Building at Johns Hopkins Hospital, where Tom had his room. We went into a room and he said, Dr. Dandy said, 'I want to tell you the patient is desperately sick.' He said, 'If it's tumor here and tumor there,' pointing to his lungs and pointing to his head, he said, 'the case is absolutely hopeless.' If it's cancer and cancer, and if it's multiple tuberculosis, it's hopeless. There's only one chance and that is a single tuberculer.' And he said, 'Then it would depend then where that is. It would have to be right back here,' and he put his hand on the back of his head. And he said, 'The chances are entirely against him.' And I said, 'Well, what chance has he? What are his chances?' He said, '95 against him.' And he said, 'Tell you what we'd like to do this afternoon is do a little trepanning.' He said, 'It would make it easier for X-rays and so forth.' So finally after we rebelled a little—Mama wanted to wait until Fred came and I felt that time was precious. Mr. Aswell felt so, too, and he went in the room where Tom was.

"And Dr. Dandy was a very gruff sort of man on the outside but a beautiful bedside manner and they all called him Tom. They all called him Tom. No one 'Mr. Wolfed' him at Baltimore except the nurses. But he said, 'Now, Tom, I've been talking to your mother and sister and Mr. Aswell,' and he said, 'we want to bore a little hole, with your permission, right back here in your head.'

The Angel made famous by Thomas Wolfe's first novel, Look Homeward Angel. The statue stood on the front porch of the tombstone shop all the years Tom was growing up in in Asheville. It is now in a cemetery in Hendersonville, N.C. Photo by Lou Harshaw

Mama had taken her place on the other side of Tom's bed where she could look right down and hold his hand and he said, 'Well, Doctor,' he said, 'you're not going to bore clean through are you?' And he said, 'Oh, no, just a little hole. You won't hardly see it. Just to let off the pressure that you have there. It's causing the severe headaches and to give us a better chance.' Well, Mama kissed him and Tom laughed and looked up at her and said 'And this goes with it, too.'

"He had it done that afternoon. I had phoned the family. Fred phoned the family. Fred got there early Sunday morning and Sunday was a terrible day. Tom was most miserable. He had two very fine brain nurses taking care of him. They'd call us and let us go in the room occasionally. He was operated on Monday morning. Mr. Perkins had come from New York. Mr. Aswell and his literary agent, Mrs. Elizabeth Morrow, were all there. And Monday morning he was operated on. It was election day. I remember it. To quiet ourselves Mr. Perkins wondered if we couldn't go some-place and have a cocktail or something. We were all just pacing and waiting for Tom to come from the operating room. Dr. Dandy had told us that the operation was to be at nine but for us not to expect any answer until 12:30. I think it is a very long operation and we didn't know hardly. But we went across . . . there wasn't any drinks served in Baltimore that day. It was election day. Nothing served, but we went over there and had coffee in a cafe, and went back to the hospital.

"About 12:30 or quarter to one, Fred said, 'Here he comes, he is coming.' We looked down the hall and here Dr. Dandy was coming along just covered in, just foaming with perspiration, as if he had been dipped in grease, and our nurse weeping, along with him. The nurse had come with us from Seattle and had been allowed to go in and see the operation. There was a theater or something for other doctors and everything. Dr. Dandy looked at us and threw both hands up and he said, 'Perfectly hopeless, multiple tuberculosis, multiple tuberculosis.' Then he said, 'It would be far better for Tom if he could go in his sleep.'

"So that was that . . . those were just nightmarish words. We certainly didn't want to hear it. We hoped for everything. We thought a miracle would happen. We knew prayer, God, someone would step in. He couldn't be taken like that. The one member of our family tribe who had come to a point of realizing what he had struggled so hard for. He was . . . he came about five-thirty that afternoon and we were called in the room from time to time to call him back. And of course, you'd go in there and there was no answer. He was helmeted like a mummy you know, and all that they did. And Dr. Dandy had told us he'd only cut enough just for laboratory purposes, that his brain was covered with tuberculosis. That the old lesions in his lungs . . . Tom evidently in his boyhood days when he had so many colds and when he grew too fast had had a touch of tuberculosis trouble and that had healed over. Dr. Dandy said as long as that remains sealed over, you're perfectly safe. But it's deadly poison when it opens. And the result would have been exactly the same. In Tom's case when it opened from a long seige of illness of pneumonia not localizing and the fever being so high, when it opened it went into the blood stream and went to the worst possible place, with the brain stopping up. The pressure was so great and well it brought on the old pneumonia. This dreadful operation and everything and direct transfusion was given him on Wednesday afternoon.

"He was in a coma then. We didn't know it. We thought all that quiet meant he was getting better. But he died at 20 minutes of six on Thursday morning, Sept. 15th. Almost 17 years ago, 1938. He was about three weeks from his 38th birthday.

"We brought him home to Asheville. He had to stay over in Baltimore a day until they could find a casket, make one metal casket large enough to contain his big figure. He'd never looked better. He'd lost a little weight but just had that rested fine look. And we brought him home to Asheville and he was buried, I believe on the 18th. He was buried on Sunday anyway. The Sunday following that, here in Riverside Cemetery at Asheville, N.C.

Mabel stopped talking then. We had been in the studio almost two hours.

There is no question of the legacy Tom Wolfe left this town. More words have been written about Tom Wolfe than any other Asheville citizen, native or adopted. He was a giant in physical stature, a giant in the literary world. Wolfe must have been viewed as something of a changeling by his family. He was unquestionably a genius. It is always difficult for genius to deal with ordinary folk. We can only imagine his frustrations, his struggle for understanding. Wolfe, the man was real. His body and the bodies of the other members of the Wolfe family lie in Riverside Cemetery. Their tombstones rise up bold and with great bulk and substance under the shadowy trees.

Wolfe brought a new direction to American literature. He made us see things we had always seen but never noticed. Was the town he created real? Those who could tell us are mostly gone now, buried in nearby graves in the same cemetery.

"Altamont," we think, was a creation Tom Wolfe fashioned from a thousand gleanings, patiently pieced together in a mosaic, perhaps unmatched in modern literature.

Our heritage as a town has been immeasurably enriched by the writings of Wolfe. He gave us a new dimension of ourselves, a fresh wind blowing over old lands. He created characters as exaggerated as his own personality must have been and threw us into his own paradox: his desire to be well known, intimately known with all the human faults and frailties, yet to be admired and respected, a feat not always possible for a person or a town.

While the people from whom he drew bits and pieces to create his characters were real, "Altamont" in *Look Homeward Angel* was not. This fact was realized but not recognized until later, much later.

Nevertheless, Tom Wolfe left for us a magnificent tapestry of ourselves, woven with an infinite number of threads in heretofore undesigned patterns of untold richness and great detail.

He was, as Mabel said, "Someone to be proud of."

"Old Kentucky Home" the boarding house in Asheville written about as "Dixieland" in Tom Wolfe's **Look Homeward Angel**. *Tom is the little boy sitting out on the step. W.O. his father in the chair in the yard, the mother is on the porch. The man in the hat on steps is undidentified. Photo courtesy Pack Memorial Library.*

CHAPTER VIII

There Are Many Heroes

THE first faint stirrings of the movement to create a large National Park west of the city seems to have come out of Franklin, North Carolina in the early 1800's.

Dr. C.D. Smith, of Franklin, in 1885, read a paper before a medical meeting in New York City about the climatic treatment of disease, and advicated the establishment of a health resort in Western North Carolina.

The paper was published in the *Journal of the American Medical Association* where it caught the attention of Dr. Chase Ambler of Ohio who read it and was so impressed that he moved his practice to Asheville. If there are heroes to be named in the establishment of the Great Smoky Mountains National Park, at the top of the list would be Dr. Ambler and Horace Kephart. But the list is long and there are many heroes.

Two more different men cannot be imagined.

Horace Kephart, son of a clergyman, came into the Smokies to recuperate from ill health, mostly alcoholism, a disease from which he never fully recovered. He was a learned man, a librarian interested in writings which concerned the western wilderness.

Kephart was also a loner, a man who found the solace of this life in the unpopulated ruggedness of the southern mountains. It was to be his two books, *Camping and Woodcraft*, a classic which gained him the title of "Grand Old Man of the Campfire and Long Trail," and *Our Southern Highlanders*, which was published in 1913 and sold 10,000 copies in the first edition. The book has since gone through several revisions and seven printings by 1957.

Kephart wrote an article in the *Asheville Times* in which he boldly proposed a national park for the mountains of North Carolina and eastern Tennessee.

When the *Asheville Times* endorsed the proposal the following day, it was in defiance of the powerful and wealthy timber interests which were rapidly taking their toll of the southern forests.

Meanwhile in Asheville, Dr. Ambler had become a prime mover in the efforts to establish a park for the region. In 1899 he organized the Appalachian National Park Association.

Author Michael Frome in his definitive and comprehensive book on the Smokies, *Strangers in High Places*, writes of a meeting that took place in George Vanderbilt's mansion in the early 1890's. Attending in addition to Vanderbilt, were state geologist of North Carolina, Dr. Joseph A. Holmes and Gifford Pinchot. Frome says, "While they sat in Mr. Vanderbilt's brick house and discussed things in general and forestry in particular, Holmes advanced a notion that the Federal Government ought to buy a big tract of timberland in the southern Appalachian and practice forestry on it. Half a century later, Pinchot credited Holmes with

149

the 'brilliant suggestion' that led to acquisition of millions of acres of land for national forests in the east."

As dedicated as the efforts were, it was to be forty years before the Great Smokies National Park became a reality.

The difficulty lay in the ownership of the lands. In the west it had been relatively easy for the Government to acquire vast unpopulated tracts which were, for the most part already under government control.

In the Smokies, the lands were under private ownership, either in tiny holdings of the mountain farmers or in the hands of lumber companies.

After long years of struggle and much wrangling at the Congressional level it remained for the two states and private enterprise to raise the major portion of the money to buy the lands.

A major hurdle for the Park was overcome when Champion Paper and Fibre Company, who owned the largest tract, 92,800 acres, including the crest of the Guyot and Clingman's Dome mountains, after much negotiation, agreed to sell all their holdings for about one fourth their original price.

Staff writer, Lucille Clark, in her fine article written for the 90th Anniversary Edition of *The Asheville Citizen*, July 17, 1960 says: "The two states raised $2,000,000 each, and private donations were accepted—notably, John D. Rockefeller's $5,000,000, the Laura Spelman Rockefeller Memorial. In 1930, 158,799 acres were deeded to the U.S.A. and use of the lands as a national park began the following year. President Roosevelt and Congress allotted $1,560,000 and $74,300 respectively, and the kitty was $12,369,693.91 when operations began. North Carolina finished its land acquisition in 1938, Tennessee later, and the final report filed in 1947 shows that North Carolina bought 229,573.01 acres in Swain and Haywood Counties for $5,821,881.34. Which certainly is different from, say Yellowstone."

On Labor Day in 1940 President Franklin D. Roosevelt, arriving with a large entourage, having driven over the mountains from Chattanooga, arriving at Newfound Gap, three-quarters of an hour late, dedicated the Park from a naturally level outcropping of the mountain. It had been enclosed by a rock wall and was large enough to hold some 20 dignitaries. Thousands gathered below on the parking lot. It was a mixed crowd. Mingling with the high placed government officials in their suits and ties were the mountain country people in their overalls and gingham dresses. From Asheville and the surrounding counties came many of the people who had worked so diligently, so long, to make the Park a reality.

One of the main characters of the drama was missing—Rockefeller. His money had been the capstone in the Park acquisition, yet as sometimes happens, those who contribute a great deal cannot, or choose not to be present to share the final triumph.

Much as the early morning mists shroud the surrounding high peaks along the Blue Ridge Parkway, the early origins of efforts to build this scenic highway are lost in the hazy passage of time.

Perhaps Sam P. Weems, superintendent of the Parkway from April 8, 1944 to July 3, 1966, says it as well as it can be stated historically in his summary prepared by him and his staff around 1960 and published in the 90th Anniversary edition of *The Asheville Citizen Times*.

"Prior to the origin of the Blue Ridge Parkway, the idea of a scenic mountain route undoubtedly existed in many minds. Prior to World War I, Colonel J.H. Pratt of the North Carolina Geologic and Economic Survey charted a route from Roanoke, Virginia through North Carolina to Greenville, South Carolina. Only one short section was completed before the war stopped it. Coincidentally, the Parkway follows portions of the old grades in the vicinity of Altapass, N.C. miles 323 to 326.

"The basic idea of a national parkway through the Blue Ridge Mountains probably occurred to a number of interested individuals, but the actual birth of the Blue Ridge Parkway seems to have been the result of spontaneous combustion.

"On August 11, 1933, President Franklin D. Roosevelt visited Shenandoah National Park on an inspection tour of CCC camps. Included in his party were Secretary of the Interior Harold Ickes, Secretary of Agriculture Henry Wallace and Senator Harry Byrd of Virginia. The President was favorably impressed by the scenery he viewed from a section of the Skyline Drive, which now extends the length of the Shenandoah National Park, and gave warm acceptance to Senator Byrd's suggestion that a scenic mountain route be constructed to connect the Shenandoah and Great Smoky Mountains National Parks. The project fitted appropriately into the program of public works Mr. Roosevelt was fostering to help turn the tide of economic depression.

"The following September a meeting of the League of Virginia Municipalities was held in Richmond. Following this event a portion of this group including Gov. G.J. Pollard, Sen. Byrd and Theodore E. Straus of the Public Works Administration met at a luncheon in the executive mansion.

"The possibility of a parkway to connect Shanandoah and Great Smoky Mountains National Parks was

The Blue Ridge Parkway is the most visited National Park area in America. The road connects the Shenandoah National Park with the Great Smoky Mountains National Park. Asheville is on the route. Photo by Lou Harshaw

A Parkway ranger gazes out over the beauty of Cone Memorial Park on milepost 292.7 north of Asheville. Photo courtesy Asheville Chamber of Commerce by Lou Harshaw

advanced in a group discussion and received the approval of Gov. Pollard. Accordingly, he appointed a Virginia committee to facilitate the matter and requested Sen. Byrd to be chairman.

"On Oct. 5, Gov. Pollard sent telegrams to Gov. J.C.B. Ehringhous of North Carolina and Gov. Hill McAlister of Tennessee, requesting them to appoint committees to cooperate with Virginia.

"A conference on the part of the Government and the interested states was held in Sen. Byrd's Washington office Oct. 7. Among those present, in addition to the Senator and the state committees, were Sen. R.R. Reynolds of North Carolina; Arno B. Cammerer, director, National Park Service; Conrad L. Wirth, assistant director; Thomas H. MacDonald, chief, Bureau of Public Roads; George L. Radcliffe, director, and Theodore E. Straus, member of the advisory board, Region 10 Public Works Administration; and Joesph Kirchner, regional forester, Eastern Region, U.S. Forest Service.

"The purpose of the meeting was 'to consider ways and means of constructing a road to connect the two great national parks, the Shenandoah National Park and Great Smoky Mountains National Park.' During the meeting Sen. Byrd stated that the idea originated with Mr. MacDonald. The latter, however, disclaimed the honor. 'It is one of the outgrowths of a conversation that has taken place with Sen. Byrd and others of Virginia and of the states that are interested and with Mr. Radcliffe and Mr. Straus of the Public Works Administration; and numerous other individuals have already taken part in bringing into a rather definite concept this whole idea.'

"He further stated . . .'if we develop a highway of this character, we would have it used by a number of people . . . beyond our comprehension.' The ever-increasing Parkway travel, now nearly six million annually, proves his prophecy.

"All the committee members favored the road. A letter was prepared submitting the proposal to Secretary Ickes, who also served as Public Works Administrator. It was to be a federal project to cost $16,600,000 for an estimated 441 miles. At this point the precise route had not been decided.

"On Nov. 18, 1933, Secretary Ickes notified Cammerer that the President had approved the proposed parkway, providing Virginia, North Carolina and Tennessee would defray the cost of location surveys and acquire and deed the right-of-way to the United States. In December, 1933, an allotment of $4,000,000 was made for the project according to provisions of the National Industry Recovery Act.

"The project was set up under the National Park Service and the Bureau of Public Roads in accordance with an existing inter-bureau agreement. Radcliffe was appointed chairman of an advisory committee to coordinate federal and state interests.

"The states were asked to submit proposed routes to the Secretary of the Interior. A general hearing was arranged in Baltimore in February, 1934. Radcliffe presided as chairman. Officials of the Bureau of Public Roads and the National Park Service were present. The governors, senators and representatives of the states presented their recommendations.

"Virginia made no specific proposals as a considerable distance of the Parkway would of necessity be located within its borders. North Carolina and Tennessee, however, favored distinctly different routes. Ultimately the North Carolina proposal was approved. Tennessee outlined a route branching westward from the present Parkway location near Linville, N.C. and entering the east side of the Great Smoky Mountains National Park via the Unaka Mountains.

"In order to evaluate the proposals of the two states, a National Park Service reconnaisance party made two trips over the territory in the spring of 1934. Consideration was given to various routes, including one that extended through a portion of West Virginia.

"In June the National Park Service and Bureau of Public Roads submitted a joint report to the Secretary of the Interior recommending the route crossing over into Tennessee. In July, 1934, the Secretary approved the route south from Shenandoah National Park at Jarman's Gap to the James River, and from Adney Gap, Va., to Blowing Rock, N.C.

"In consequence of concerted activity by North Carolina under the leadership of R. Getty Browning, chief state locating engineer, a second hearing was arranged by the Secretary in September, 1934. In November the Parkway route was definitely established by the Secretary from Blowing Rock to Great Smoky Mountains National Park in general accord with the North Carolina recommendations. The route between James River and Roanoke developed as a natural result of the locations approved by the Secretary, although there was no specific defining statement issued.

"The basic act giving statutory reality to the Parkway was passed on June 30, 1936, H.R. 12455, number 848, by the 74th Congress. No data are presently available on the sponsors or the relevant speeches,

MOUNT MITCHELL STATE PARK
HIGHEST POINT IN EASTERN AMERICA

PICNICKING · CAMPING
HIKING · PARK MUSEUM
RESTAURANT OPEN MAY - OCT.

NORTH CAROLINA
DEPARTMENT OF CONSERVATION AND DEVELOPMENT
DIVISION OF STATE PARKS

Mount Mitchell, northeast of Asheville is the highest peak in the Eastern United States. Richard Brown of Pack Memorial Library at Asheville tells us that there are 48 peaks in the State which reach 6,000 feet or over. George W. McCoy's book, **Official Data on Western North Carolina's Highest Peaks** *published by the* **Asheville Citizen-Times** *supplies this and other detailed information on the mountains. Photograph courtesy Asheville Chamber of Commerce by Bob Lindsey*

The Southern Appalachians (below) which surround Asheville on all sides make it a true mountain metropolis. The city is on the route of the Blue Ridge Parkway and east of the Great Smoky Mountains National Park. Photo by Lou Harshaw

if any, made in Congress. This date is the origin of the name, 'Blue Ridge Parkway.' Formerly it was referred to as the Appalachian Parkway and as the Shenandoah to Great Smoky Mountains Parkway.

"The National Park Service realized from the first stages of actual Parkway planning and construction that it did not have anyone familiar with the Parkway type of development and accordingly went to the Westchester (N.Y.) County Parkway organization for an experienced landscape architect.

"On Dec. 26, 1933, Stanley W. Abbott was appointed resident landscape architect and given practically a blanket ticket of instructions. Landscape architects Edward H. Abbuehl and H.E. van Gilder soon joined him to make up the Parkway field staff that for one year covered the entire Parkway territory and made frequent trips to Washington.

"In January, 1935, the Bureau of Public Roads moved its Luray, Virginia office to Roanoke, and the Parkway also established an office there in the same building. From this time on, the organization grew rapidly.

"In the spring of 1937 Abbott was designated acting superintendent and resident landscape architect, and that summer the ranger force was started with R.A. Wagoner as deputy park ranger. In the fall Sam P. Weems was advanced from project manager for the purchase and development of recreation areas and associated project, to the post of assistant superintendent in 1944.

"As of 1960 the Parkway has 135 permanent positions. They are: engineering, construction, and maintenance, 76; protection, 29; administrative, fiscal and clerical, 25; landscape architects, 1; soil conservationist, 1; interpretation, 3."

Superintendent Weems only hints at the tremendous controversy that blew ill winds over North Carolina and Tennessee in years of dispute over the route of the Parkway. Nor does the report mention the difficulties that arose between the state of North Carolina and the Cherokee Indians in the routing of the Parkway over the Qualla Reservation.

If the Blue Ridge Parkway is a "thing of beauty" at the present time when it is completed with the exception of one small link around Grandfather Mountain, the convulsions of controversy that arose during its birthing and that have periodcally developed since, have caused bitter rifts both between community factions and between the Government and local communities.

Two proposals in the late 1950's resulted in tremendous public opposition. The proposal by Parkway officials to expand Government owned lodging facilities in the Parkway and the proposal to put a toll on the road were defeated by the concerted efforts of Chamber of Commerce groups and other interested organizations and individuals. It was also about this time that the battle over the route around Grandfather Mountain, a popular privately owned tourist attaction, came to a head and was finally resolved. This last section which is to be a first in methods of engineering and construction in the country, promises to be one of the most beautiful stretches of road on the Parkway.

Despite early controversies there seems no question of the tremendous impact the Parkway and the Great Smoky Mountains National Park have had on the city.

As Phyllis Vance, Manager Membership and Communications Department of the Asheville Chamber of Commerce says: "Asheville's close proximity to the spectacular Blue Ridge Parkway and the Great Smoky Mountains National Park makes the city a natural headquarters from which to sample the 'Land of the Sky.'

"Many visitors come to the Asheville area to find accommodations ranging from rustic to modern and use the city as a base to take several one day trips to various points along the Parkway. Other visitors who are traveling in the national parks, come to the Asheville area to find lodging, to sample the variety of restaurants, to enjoy one of the many attractions, to see native crafts and to buy everything from picnic supplies to gasoline for their vehicles.

"During 1979, over six million visitors traveled by Milepost 382 on the Blue Ridge Parkway just east of Asheville at Oteen. The Great Smokies continued to be the nation's most visited national park. The North Carolina Travel Revenue Survey, based on hotel/motel revenues, shows that travel revenue for Buncombe County in 1979 was $143.9 million.

"Although an exact figure is not available, it is only logical to believe that a good portion of these travel dollars comes from the millions of visitors who travel the Blue Ridge and the Great Smokies each year."

The Southern Highlands Handicraft Guild's Folk Art Center is located on the Blue Ridge Parkway at Asheville and is co-sponsored with the Parkway. The Center features the handicraft of the region. Photo by Lou Harshaw

CHAPTER IX

A Crowd of Two Thousand Watched

No book about Asheville would be complete without an accounting of how important religion has been down through the years.

The earliest congregation seems to be one that was organized before the village really came into existence. There were several small groups meeting for religious worship in the surrounding settlements but the oldest one within the boundaries of the future city was established in 1794.

The tiny group was composed of Scotch-Irish Presbyterians that came into the mountains after the Revolutionary War. These settlers came into the Swannanoa Valley and into the Bee Tree Creek area about 1785. In the following few years they built what became known as Robert Patton's Meeting House.

The Scotch-Irish settlement grew westward down the Swannanoa to the French Broad River and into the Reems and Hominy Creek Valleys.

The Scotch—Irish Presbyterians established an academy in 1793 about one half mile north of the Swannanoa River near the present Biltmore. It was here in a one room log building that Robert Henry, a Revolutionary patriot taught in the first school west of the Blue Ridge Mountains, but also the first religious meetings were to be held that would be within the confines of the future city.

The little school was first called Union Hill and then Union Hill Academy.

In 1797, the Rev. George Newton served as headmaster and as minister to the congregation.

Newton migrated on westward into Tennessee in 1814, and the records seem to be dim as to the activity of the church and school until 1837, when James Patton and Col. Samuel Chunn worked out a proposal whereby they deeded land on Church Street for a building.

Funds were raised and the First Presbyterian Church building was erected in 1841 at a cost of $4,000. The church building faced east and was reached by a wooden bridge from what is now Biltmore Avenue.

During the early years in this building the church thrived and grew under the leadership of several distinguished ministers.

In 1884-1885, the first church building was taken down and under the leadership of the Rev. Knox Polk Gammon the nave of the present building went up. The structure was turned around to face west and the entrance was now on Church Street. The gothic tower and spire is one of the city's most enduring and beloved landmarks.

Among the church's most distinguished ministers was the Rev. Robert Fishburne Campbell who served the congregation for more than 54 years until his death on April 3, 1947.

It almost could be said that the history of the church's growth and strength during this period is the story of Dr. Campbell's inspired ministry.

Grace Episcopal Church, or Beaverdam Mission as it was known then, was founded in 1867 primarily through the efforts of three men: the Reverend Jarvis Buxton, first rector of Trinity Episcopal Church in Asheville; Frank J. Murdock, lay reader at Trinity and later an ordained minister; and General James Green Martin, Civil War hero and also a lay reader at Trinity. These men decided on the location of the mission and raised money from donation for the construction of a log chapel. The land and the logs were the gift of Professor John Kimberly. Murdock was lay reader and first Superintendent of the Sunday School of the mission. Other teachers and workers in the early days were Captain T.W. Patton, Miss Fanny Patton, Miss Kate Buxton, and a number of the Kimberly family, including Misses Emma, Rebecca, Mary Fannie, and Mr. and Mrs. Maney Kimberly. Dr. Buxton came out from Asheville twice a month to hold services.

By the 1880's the mission was no longer called "Beaver Dam Mission" but "Grace Mission" or "Grace Chapel,"the name coming from the little community of Grace, two miles from Asheville, in which the chapel was located. Also by this time a rectory had been built, a priest, the Reverend W.F. Rice, had been brought in to serve the church, and the church had been established as an Organized Mission of the Diocese of Western North Carolina.

Father Rice, assisted for several years by the Reverend A.H. Stubbs of the Ravenscroft Associate Mission, served the church until his retirement in 1907. It was in the 90's also that Mrs. C. T. Chester and her daughter, Susan, (later Mrs. Chester Lyman) moved into the community and became affiliated with the mission. It was largely the results of their efforts that a drive for a new church building culminated in the construction of the present stone church building, construction beginning in August of 1905. The new church was designated as a memorial church, where memorials could be established in memory of relatives or others as specified by donors to the building fund. Donations were received from as far away as New York City, including one from Grace Church of New York in memory of William F. Chester. For many years the church was known as Grace Memorial Episcopal Church.

The above information was supplied by Philip A. Walker. Photograph by Lou Harshaw

Small community church (at left) near Bakersville north of Asheville. Photo by Lou Harshaw

159

The long awaited dedication of the First Presbyterian Church was held January 25, 1903 after completion of the Sunday School building.

After the retirement of Dr. Campbell, Dr. Calvin Grier Davis became pastor and served until October of 1959 when he left the church to become president of the Mountain Retreat Association and of Montreat-Anderson College.

The impressive complex of large buildings that is the First Baptist Church had its humble beginnings on February 28, 1829 when four people came together on a hillside above the French Broad River to meet in religious worship. They were Swan Burnett and his wife, Frances, and Thomas Stradley and Elizabeth Gasperson.

There had been Baptists in the area prior to 1802, but these four meeting in the Burnett Home, taking part in services led by Stradley, deserve special recognition. For it was from this group with its growth and expansion that was to be the foundation of the future First Baptist Church.

For three years the group met at the Burnett home on the first Saturdays and Sundays of each month. Later Stradley's brother Peter and his wife Naomi were accepted into the church and baptized in the river below.

By December of that first year, their number had grown to 11 people and with the assistance of Isaac

One of the most outstanding churches in the downtown area is Mount Zion Missionary Baptist Church. Its many towers and art glass windows make it a truly handsome building. Photo by Lou Harshaw

Since this picture was taken, there have been two or three additions to the Central Methodist Church on Church Street. Every effort has been made to keep the architecture harmonious. Photo courtesy The Ball Collection, Southern Highlands Research Center, Asheville

Mills of Newfound Baptist Church, they organized themselves into Mount Pleasant Baptist Church. Swan Burnett and Peter Stradley were chosen as deacons.

In August of 1830, the little congregation was admitted into the French Broad Association and Thomas Stradley was ordained to be the first pastor of the "Baptist Church of Asheville."

Stradley had migrated from England in 1828 and, after living in the Asheville mountain village for five years, had moved up on a Beaverdam farm where he opened up a blacksmith shop and raised 13 children.

The records show that Stradley, after riding red clay roads in all kinds of weather back and forth to town to preach each month, received $21 in gifts. It was the year 1858.

In 1831, the group had been called together to clear ground on the old Turnpike in order to build a permanent meeting house.

The small structure was built on borrowed land on old Patton Avenue, now West Haywood Street. It was a log building which, when the land it was standing on was sold out from under it in later years, brought a total of $20 to the congregation.

The log cabin meeting house, however, when completed in 1832, was dedicated by the 29 members. Seven of these were men.

One of the main problems with the church was that this first permanent home was too far out of town and for the next 30 years the services remained small.

The members were forced to seek new quarters in 1861 and moved into the basement, all that was completed at the time, of a little church at Spruce and Woodfin Streets.

The Civil War halted construction until finally in 1871, Stradley put up his Beaverdam farm as security and funds were raised for its completion. At one point, the church doors were nailed closed by the contractor to whom money was still owed.

"Father Stradley" retired from active service to the church in 1875 when he was at last able to see it on

161

Snowflakes accentuate the roof pattern of All Souls Episcopal Church in Biltmore. The church was built by George Vanderbilt and consecrated on November 8, 1896 by Bishop Joseph Cheshire. The church was designed by Richard Hunt in the early Gothic style of churches in Northern England. Photo by Dick Harshaw

162

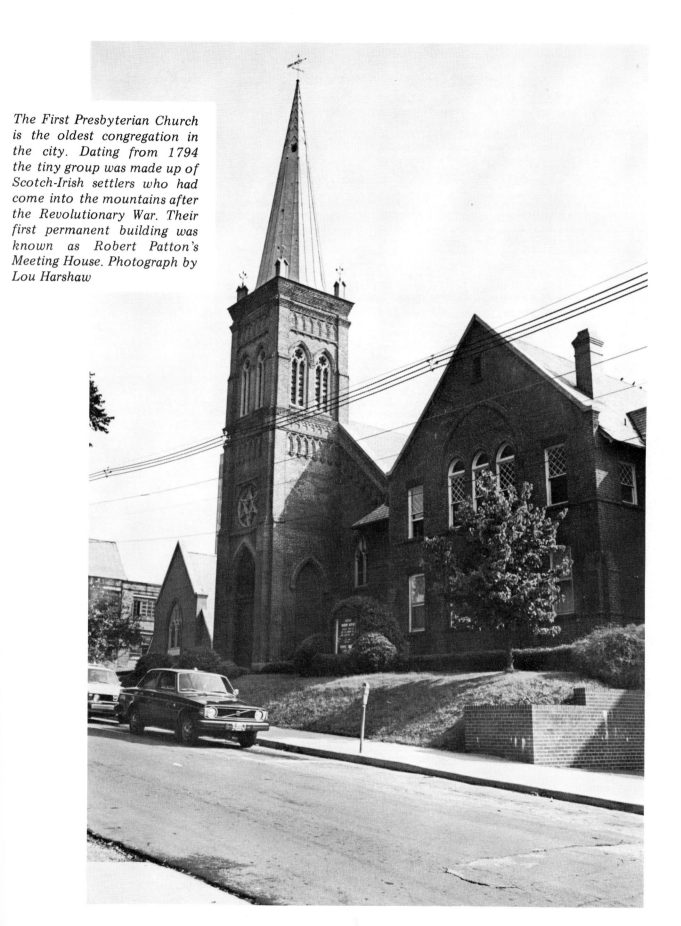

The First Presbyterian Church is the oldest congregation in the city. Dating from 1794 the tiny group was made up of Scotch-Irish settlers who had come into the mountains after the Revolutionary War. Their first permanent building was known as Robert Patton's Meeting House. Photograph by Lou Harshaw

a sound financial footing, although it still needed some help from the State Baptist Mission Board to pay the minister. Stradley was succeeded by Dr. John Mitchell of Murfreesboro.

The next year the Rev. F.M. Jordan held a revival and 33 new members were added. They were baptized in the waters of the French Broad River while a crowd of 2000 watched.

Four years later the church had grown to the point where a full time minister could be hired. Dr. A.C. Dixon came to head the church and received $600 a year. It was later increased to $1,000. Dr. Dixon was a brilliant man, an inspired leader, who was listed in *Who's Who in America*. During his pastorate, the church grew by several hundred members.

During Asheville's first boom period when the railroads came in the church membership went over the 500 mark.

The residences of yesterday cluster in close to First Baptist Church. At the present time these have all been cleared away and the road rerouted to make way for the Beaucatcher cut and the connector highway bypass No. 240 skirting this area. Photo courtesy The Ball Collection, Southern Highlands Research Center, Asheville

A new church building at the corner of Spruce and College Streets was completed in 1882 and a dedication was held. The total cost was $30,000, most of which was borrowed. This was to lead the church into another financial crisis when the panic of 1892 hit and for the next ten years, the church struggled to repay the debt which with interest came to $40,000.

However, the church membership continued to grow and reached 2,000 people under the leadership of Dr. W.M. Vines.

By the early 1920's the College Street building was overcrowded and the membership launched its most ambitious expansion program under Dr. Robert Bateman, then serving as minister.

Ground was broken on November 16, 1925 for the present distinctive building at Oak and Woodfin Streets. It was completed at a cost of $70,000 with the dedication being held on March 6, 1927. Its cost reflected the inflationary values of Asheville's second boom period, but did not seem excessive for the large congregation at that time. The church was to suffer along with the rest of the town in the depression and it was not until 1944 and the appointment of Dr. W. Perry Crouch that a new and successful campaign was begun which freed the church of indebtedness at last in 1951.

Several remodelings and expansions have since taken place and the church is even now undergoing an extensive building program.

No writing on religion in the mountains of Western North Carolina would be complete without mention of that most dedicated of all ministers of the gospel, Francis Asbury.

Asbury was born in England in 1745, the son of one of John Wesley's earliest and most ardent followers. He became a Methodist when he was 13 years old and was preaching to local groups at 16. He became a fulltime minister at the age of 22. Wesley sent Asbury to America in 1771 in order to do missionary work.

With the motto: "To love God and bring others to do so," Asbury began what was to be one of the most difficult, most dedicated Christian ministries in America.

He became a "circuit rider" traveling a regular route in the backwoods of the Southern Appalachians, ministering to his small congregations once a month as he could get to them.

On horseback he was on the trails constantly and soon earned the title "Prophet of the Long Road." He spent so much time on his horse that he wrote his sermons on horseback and some even said he learned to sleep in the saddle while his trusted steed picked the way cautiously over the mountain paths.

He was made a Bishop at age 39.

Francis Asbury first came into Western North Carolina in 1789 from Tennessee. He made his first trip to Buncombe County November 9, 1800.

Fortunately, Bishop Asbury kept meticulous diaries, writing down his entries as he rode, perhaps. From them, we know he visited George Swain (father of Governor David Swain) and the Daniel Killian home in the Beaverdam section. The Killian house later was torn down and the property was bought by Capt. Victor Baird, grandfather of Mrs. Ray Cagle. She and her husband now have a home on the land located on Elk Mountain Scenic Highway.

Asbury also visited the home of Col. James Lowry on Sandy Mush Creek. He preached frequently around the Mills River and the Davidson River areas.

In Asheville he stayed with Andrew Erwin who was, later, to become Asheville's first postmaster.

In 1832, Daniel Killian deeded the land on which the Asbury Memorial United Methodist Church now stands at 171 Beaverdam Road. The land had been obtained by him from a grant by the King of England. Actually, the church came into existence much earlier. The first building was of logs and named Beaverdam Methodist Church. During the Civil War, soldiers camped in the log church.

This original building was torn down in 1879 and a one room frame was erected. Since the building was at the foot of Mt. Pleasant, the name was changed to Mt. Pleasant Methodist Church.

In 1927, the frame structure was torn down and the present building was erected. The name was changed to Asbury Memorial. This church was officially organized by Bishop Asbury on October 11, 1801, and if not the first, certainly one of the first, to be organized as a result of Bishop Asbury's work.

Central Methodist Church has been in existence for 143 years, meeting in only three different buildings during that time.

The church was established in 1837 as a result of the work of Bishop Asbury. The first church to be built in the village, the building stood on Church Street, remarkably the same ground upon which the present building stands.

The first floor was used for classrooms and a room on the east end was used for a saddle room since most of those who attended lived too far away to walk and rode horseback.

Saddles and riding skirts were stored during the services in foul weather.

Three congregations, Presbyterian, Baptists and Methodists worshipped in the old wooden Methodist church since it was the only church building in the community.

A school for girls was conducted in the basement of the church.

Candles were used for lighting. They were made by Mrs. Jimmy Lusk, who also made the bread for communion.

The land was originally owned by J.M. Alexander. Alexander gave the land as a gift to William Coleman, Isaac Baird, Willie Jones, J.F.E. Hardy, Nicholas W. Woodfin, George W. Jones, James Smith, Joshua Roberts and himself, all of whom were designated trustees.

St. Lawrence Church dedicated in 1909 has the largest Catholic congregation in Western North Carolina. The architect was Rafael Guastavino who came to the mountains of Western North Carolina to work on the construction of Biltmore House. Photograph by Lou Harshaw

The Rev. J.S. Burnett was the first fulltime pastor. When he took office there were 60 white members and 59 black members.

In 1857, the frame church was replaced by brick. It had two entrance doors, two aisles, four high windows on each side, four columns on the front, and a square steeple. A small flue stove was used for heating.

A bell was purchased by the Ladies Sewing Circle for $138 and placed in the tower. It was used every service to call the members to church. The building also contained a basement and balconies.

This building was remodeled several times to add a minister's study, a Sunday school, and prayer meeting rooms over the vestibule.

A fence was constructed in front of the church in 1870.

At first, a small organ was used to provide music but was later replaced by a "Felgemaker," a larger hand pumped instrument. Often during services, old "Adam," the sexton, was prone to doze off and had to be awakened in order to provide the hand power to the pump for the music for the closing hymn.

The records show that in 1879 the estimated value of the church was $3,500. The parsonage was worth $2,000. By 1882, church value had increased to $10,000 and the parsonage was valued at $3,000. Enrollment was 310.

The minister's salary in 1876 was $900 per year; by 1882 it had gone up to $1,000.

The land for the first parsonage was donated by W.D. Rankin in 1877.

The minister's home was erected by the Women's Sewing Society and was almost surrounded by graveyards. It was across Aston Street at the Episcopal Church and on the west side where a Methodist cemetery had been established in 1865. The remains were removed in 1885 to Riverside Cemetery.

In 1899, when the Rev. J.W. Weaver was appointed head of the congregation, he began a campaign to raise money for a new church. Property west of the church was donated in 1901 to the trustees by Mrs. Mattie A. Johnson, W.T. Weaver and Annie L. Weaver, to be used for church purposes.

Trustees were M.J. Bearden, James P. Sawyer, R.H. Reeves, J.M. Ingles, F. Stikeleather, E.C. Chambers and W.R. Whitson.

The name had been changed to Central Methodist Church.

The first stone in the foundation was laid in the fall of 1902 when a simple service was held.

By Aug. 25, 1903, in an opening behind a limestone tablet at the rear of the loggia, a copper box 11 inches x 6 inches, which contained certain important church documents depicting church history to that time, was placed.

It was well that these were preserved. The city auditorium where the congregation had been meeting burned to the ground, destroying all church property except a small widow's mite box and the offering plates.

The first service in the new church was held November 5, 1905. It had cost $90,000. The old city firebell was placed in the tower, where it remains today. The old bell has been rung on several occasions to commemorate historical events at the church.

According to records, one lone Episcopalian, Henrietta Kerr Patterson, lived within the town limits in 1847. She was a South Carolinian from Charleston. Her husband, James W. Patton, was the son of staunch Presybterian Scotsmen from North Ireland. Another Episcopalian lady, Ann Evelina Baird Coleman, the second wife of William Coleman, lived in the "old Coleman House" (burned in 1933) on Weaverville Road. According to the book *Trinity Episcopal Church* by Wanda Engle Stanard and Emily Schubert Carr, they quote another source: " 'For years she rode a white mule to church with a darky following along behind on another mule'."

The third member of this group was Salena Corpening Roberts. She and her husband Philetus were the parents of Julia Bethel Roberts Clayton (Mrs. Ephraim, S.), who was Trinity's oldest member until her death in 1959.

It was these three who confronted Bishop Ives when he visited Asheville on August 15, 1858. Impressed by the ladies, he made plans for regular services to be held. He chose Jarvis Buxton from Rutherfordton for the missionary priest.

According to the book on Trinity: "Every second Sunday Jarvis Buxton rode horseback from Rutherfordton to Ahseville by way of Hickory Nut Gap—a seemingly endless 41 miles. Early in this churchless period services were held in the lobby of the Eagle Hotel, located on the east side of South Main near Eagle Street and owned by James W. Patton. '. . . this house in its early days was considered the best kept hotel between Lexington, Ky. and Charleston, S.C. and was a famous stopping place for the traveling community.'

So wrote an old timer Albert T. Summey. Hotel rates around that time, $7.00 to $8.00 a month; candles and fuel extra."

The Episcopalian group next chose to meet in the large upper room of the Asheville Female College on Oak Street.

But the congregation acutely felt the need for their own building. Frank Wills of New York was chosen as architect to draw plans in the Pointed Style brick that would seat about 200. Ephraim Clayton, an experienced builder who had also constructed the historic county courthouse at Dahlonega, Georgia (now the oldest public building still in use in North Georgia), oversaw the work which was started in 1849, and Col. Philetus Wallcott Roberts was the contractor. James W. Patton donated the land on the corner of Church and Aston Streets.

The church was completed July 1, 1850, and was consecrated by Bishop Ives July 6, 1851.

By 1869 the neat Gothic church was proving too small for the growing congregation, and it was announced that subscriptions for a new church would be taken.

In 1870 Trinity Parish, under the guidance of Dr. Buxton, had established the first school for Black people. It was located on Valley Street.

The cornerstone for the new church, which was to be built on the same site, was laid in 1881. The cost was to be $8,000. According to the city directory of that day, it was "an elegant and commodius structure."

On the night of November 15, 1910, a disastrous fire broke out at Trinity. The clanging of the fire bells brought out crowds of people running from all directions. It was thought sparks from a faulty flue set the furnace room ablaze.

From the book on Trinity: "City firemen were unable to check the fire and by morning the church was a blackened shell. The chancel arch was still intact, but the stained glass windows shattered; the baptismal font, a memorial to Miss Joesphine Buel broken from its marble base. Dozens of other memorials and gifts were destroyed. *The Asheville Citizen*'s comment 'The loss of so fine an edifice is greatly to be deplored . . . . Beneath its roof some of the most famous figures in national history have worshipped'."

The following night a meeting was held, and after Haywood Parker made a brief but convincing plea, the men of the church resolved "that we rebuild Trinity Church at once."

The cornerstone was laid on All Saints Day in 1911, but the rebuilding was to proceed slowly. The estimated cost was $50,000. The new church was completed in 1913, when a note was sent to Mr. Lord (the architect) for his work in designing and supervising the building of the church.

Saint Lawrence Church was dedicated in October of 1909. Its unusual architecture has been an Asheville landmark since its completion. The church has the largest Catholic congregation in the Western part of the state.

The body of its architect, Rafael Guastavino, rests in a crypt in the church. He died during the construction of the church, and his work was carried on under the supervision of his son.

Asheville is a city of stately old churches. As the congregations grew in size and moved on to other newer and larger locations, the empty buildings were soon occupied again by newly organized church groups. As the downtown churches grew in number of members, and additions were made to original buildings, great care was taken to keep these additions in harmony with the existing structures.

There are few if any empty church buildings in or near the city. While the percentage of church membership in the total population might not be as high as it once was, the church life of Asheville is still strong and healthy. There is a great deal of evidence that the powerful early influence of the Scotch-Irish Presbyterians, the circuit riding Methodists, the missionary Baptists, and the others: the Catholics who came in and established excellent schools, and the Episcopalians who were so strong in their beliefs, still exists. In addition to the Christian churches, the community has built and supports two large synagogues, Beth Ha-Tephila on North Liberty Street, a Reform Jewish congregation and Beth Israel Orthodox congregation on Murdock Avenue.

There is one Greek congregation, Holy Trinity Greek Orthodox Church on Cumberland Avenue, and one First Church of Christ Scientists on French Broad Avenue.

Each of the major denominations has established a summer retreat in the nearby mountains—the Baptists at Ridgecrest, the Methodists at Lake Junaluska, the Presbyterians at Montreat and the Episcopalians at Kanuga Conference Center near Hendersonville.

The large percentage of church members in the city has, over the years, given the community a certain stability. This is one of the, but not by any means the only, causes for a conservative viewpoint. Each generation has tended to fret somewhat at what they might term the city's "lack of progressiveness," but there is merit in the city's traditional attitude of "progressing carefully." There are those who do prefer a smaller, quieter community.

For a time after World War II, the young people moved away from the Southern Appalachians seeking better jobs and a more exciting lifestyle. In more recent years, the region has drawn in a great number of younger people who find a refuge not available in the larger calamitous metropolitan areas.

In 1832 Daniel Killian deeded the land on which the Asbury Memorial United Church now stands on Beaverdam Road. The church is one of the first congregations of the area. Photo by Lou Harshaw

CHAPTER X

The Stone Strength of the Past

SURELY the visitor who pauses long enough to drive around Asheville must, if there is a historical curiosity at all, wonder at some of the old names.

During its existence, Asheville has absorbed seven smaller villages. To the north of the main village, the small settlement of Ramoth was incorporated in 1889, and its name changed to Woolsey in 1903. Victoria was incorporated in 1887, Kenilworth in 1891, Montford and Biltmore in 1893, and South Biltmore in 1895.

West Asheville was incorporated in 1913 and was taken into the city in 1917. A portion of Woolsey was taken into the city limits in 1905, and at the same time Montford and Victory were also included.

Asheville city limits were extended in 1929 to take in Kenilworth, Biltmore, part of Biltmore Forest, a portion of South Biltmore, part of Haw Creek, part of Chunn's Cove, and an area to the north including the rest of Woolsey and a part of Lake View Park.

Buncombe had originally been formed from a part of Burke County and a part of Rutherford County to the south.

J.M. Westall served as Woolsey's only mayor until the town was absorbed into Asheville. C.T.V. Long was one of the mayors of Ramoth, and Judge J.P. Kitchen was the last mayor to serve the town of Biltmore.

Richard Thornton of the Revitalization Commission, speaking as an architect having studied carefully the history of the buildings in Asheville, says: "George Vanderbilt brought in 400 artisans and architects. When the building of the estate was completed, many artisans stayed on as did some of the architects. Their work in town resulted in such high styled buildings as St. Lawrence Church and the YMI.

"Pritchard Park took on a decided English feeling because of these outside influences.

"The more important buildings became self conscientious of prevailing architectural styles.

"Then began 20 years of a 20th century mixture of pragmatism and high style. Because brick was the primary building matieral, the mixture seemed to blend well.

"The 20's began a final historical phase with the construction of several buildings in the outstanding Art Deco style.

"Most of these were designed by the famous architect Douglas Ellington. Some of these were the S & W Building, City Hall, and the First Baptist Church. These additions continued a harmonious street-scape begun in the earlier era.

"Toward the end of the 20's a major Urban Renewal project began around on the east side of Pack

171

Square. This cleared the plaza for the new city and county buildings. The result was to destroy the European feeling of Pack Square by removing one of its walls . . . the old City Hall and Market.

"The most recent development phase of the city began with the Urban Renewal projects of the 1960's and 70's in which substantial areas east of downtown were cleared and redeveloped to create an office park. This construction was totally alien to the existing urban fabric of the city and was built for automobiles, not pedestrians.

"In the late 40's and 50's several buildings were torn down to make level parking lots. This tended to loosen up downtown, but the effects were not disastrous. Some of these gaps will be filled with new development of downtown buildings of similar scale. Some multi-story structures will be scattered throughout.

"Currently, the most important activity downtown is the construction of the Akzona, Inc, headquarters designed by I.M. Pei and several hunded thousand dollars in plazas, parks, fountains and trees around it jointly funded by City and County."

As Asheville slowly began to recover from the crushing depression of the late 1920's and early 1930's, the "saving grace," so to speak, was the tourist business. But the passing years and the coming of the automobile had brought great changes to the business. The family car propelled America into a rapid mobility

heretofore undreamed of. To accommodate the new generation, highly infected with the wanderlust fever, more "tourist homes" were opened in the downtown section and out on the highways tourist "cabins" sprang up. At first these were designed as individual units to be as quaint in style as possible. The structures were one room and a bath; sometimes cooking facilities were available in the rooms. Along the more removed highways in the mountains, some of these cabins are still in operation. They were cheap in cost, fun to stay in and made mountain travel easily affordable for a whole new group, the middle income family with several children who could come into the mountains for a week's vacation away from factory work and the hot flatlands.

Of course, these early rustic individual cabins were to gradually attach themselves together in a row to save building costs, and as the middle income traveling society became more affluent, the large luxury hotels suffered and faded out. Even the families with plenty of money preferred the convenience of being able to drive right up to the door of their room, park the car and carry in what part of the luggage was needed for the night. Also, there was the matter of clothes. The traveling American could now dress in casual, comfortable clothes without the fuss of dressing for dinner.

Two activities, both started by the Asheville Chamber of Commerce in the 1920's to aid tourism, were the Rhododendron Festival (1920) and The Mountain Dance and Folk Festival, started the year before in the baseball park to provide mountain musicians and dancers with a "stage" upon which to perform.

The Rhododendron Festival was a masterfully coordinated week-long carnival of festivities with activities, ranging from a gala high society ball to a different kind of street parade, to interest everyone every day. It drew thousands but was discontinued with the outbreak of World War II and was never revived. The Mountain Dance and Folk Festival has become nationally known and thrives on beginning "along about sundown" each evening for three nights during the first part of August.

True, the graceful life of luxury of the resort hotel was still cherished by many, but gradually these hotels were becoming fewer and fewer. While it was nice to be met by the friendly smile of the doorman who knew your name, parked your car for you, held the door and carried your many pieces of luggage, it was expensive, and newly affluent middle class Americans also had other expensive items they desired to add to their lifestyle.

Like the style of American's cars, however, the motels got bigger and better. The cabins became three, four and seven story Holiday Inns and it was again necessary, if you wanted to live in these fine surroundings, to hire a porter to carry your bags. Swimming pools and T.V. sets became a part of the required facilities. Air conditining became a necessity even in the "cool" Southern Appalachians.

Easy mobility, the coming of the air age and the new booming industries of the South brought a new kind of travel business that was to aid both the still existing luxury hotels and bring them back to life, and the large motels. It was the growing convention business which would bring in a group ranging from fifty to many thousands. The purpose could be social, political or an industrial training session, but for whatever reason, conventions were to be the salvation of the business of travel to the city.

Fortunately, the Asheville Chamber of Commerce recognized these trends early on and began an intensive promotional campaign. The promotional campaign for the general tourist business, which the Chamber had carried on since it was first organized, were kept up and intensified.

It was too late for the George Vanderbilt Hotel and the Battery Park, both of which had a number of disadvantages, such as not enough parking and no swimming facilities. The Vanderbilt became apartments for senior citizens. The Battery Park is in the process of being converted for the same purpose at the present time.

Pack Square at the present time is undergoing great change. The new Akzona Building on the right will replace the northern "wall" of brick buildings. The entire Square will be given a landscaping face lift. Photo by Lou Harshaw

The Beaucatcher Cut which will create an outlet to Interstate route 40 for the congested traffic out of the city going east. Photo by Lou Harshaw

The second World War had drawn a lot of new people into the Asheville area when it was necessary to disperse a number of government agencies out of Washington.

New energetic blood came into the city. Some of the people would remain as citizens because they liked the city or because their agencies would remain here. Others would go back to other parts of the country to spread the word about what a "nice" place Asheville was to visit or to live in. Oteen Hospital was to get more than its share of injured young men, and the U.S. Government would build a temporary hospital, Moore General, at Swannanoa to take care of the overflow. Grove Park Inn was taken over to house high-ranking German prisoners. The Arcade Building was utilized by the National Government. The weather and communications wings of the Air Force took over City Hall. Downtown hotels became redistribution centers.

After the war, Grove Park Inn was renovated.

During the war and immediately after, several new industries moved into the Buncombe County area, making it possible for the young people to find jobs. As the young soldiers returned home from fighting overseas, they began to seek out homes for their families. The outlying real estate developments, left with great empty fields after the crash, began to be bought and filled with middle to upper income family housing. Suddenly there was a new-structure housing boom on, such as the city had never experienced before.

It was also about this time that Asheville began attracting a great many retired people. This movement was promoted to a great extent by real estate developer Jack Barfield in his work for the Chamber of Commerce and gave the economy a boost of new money when it was badly needed.

The downtown section of the city, more or less static since the 1930's, suddenly began building again in the 1950's. The Northwestern Bank Building went up on the Square and this led to other new bank buildings, among them Wachovia and the Bank of Asheville (now North Carolina National Bank), which was rebuilt on the same site when their building burned on April 22, 1969. The Clyde Savings and Loan erected a handsome building on the site of the old YMCA.

Interstate route 40 crosses Biltmore Estate. Photo by Lou Harshaw

In recent years opportunities as well as problems have presented themselves to the city fathers. The voting in of the "mixed drinks" law on January 16, 1979, after a bitter battle between mainly the religious and travel groups, was to change the character of the tourist business once again. A number of fine restaurants would open in the city and the "night life" would take on a more festive air. Haute Cuisine would draw crowds to the city where they would find eating places of all different kinds.

The high cost of gasoline would start a move (admittedly slow at the present time) back to the large old houses within the city. They were to provide an answer for the incoming young families, eager to do their own renovation. A number of the old neighborhoods are being rescued from their long period of decay. The high cost of building new houses has aroused the banks and other money market sources into providing new methods of financing.

As this book is being written, almost all the problems that face other cities of this size are facing Asheville. The move to the suburbs in other years has hurt the city, but forces of change around us portend a return to downtown.

But on the other hand, Asheville as it always has, enjoys many advantages. The national population trend is to move to the Southern Sunbelt. The question is how to grow and thrive, but not lose our valuable heritage. How to maintain our quality of life, an ongoing, ever present decision-making process.

Asheville, along with the rest of the country, is at a crossroads and there are again tough questions that must be faced and answered.

A human life may be allowed only one destiny before the faint flame is snuffed out by inexorable time.

A city is different. It may have many chances at many destinies. Asheville has had its share. Its history is like a huge, panoramic painting that has been worked on for over two hundred years by hundreds of artists. Some have been tremendously talented and have painted for the ages with bold strokes and an unfaltering hand, the colors brilliant, the patterns clearly discernible.

In other times, in other years, the artistry reflects ineptness, when the painter stood too close to the canvas, perhaps, and dipped with uncleaned brush to stroke with uncertain motion, forming a dark and moody landscape filled with black shadows and a jumble of confused images.

But we only see these intermittent mistakes as we stand away from the canvas and look back on it.

So it is with history. For the most part, we are able to determine the mistakes only in retrospect.

In this time, when our concern for the future is perhaps greater than it has ever been, a time when the world in our lifetime has changed from one that we thought of as everlasting, might now by our hands be destroyed by machines we have invented. We might do well to study the past, to look at some of our mistakes, but also to determine what has enhanced the human race.

It might be that on this threshold, with a time of vital decisions approaching, a look at our city's past might enrich its future.

As Robert Jeffers said in *To the Rock that Will Be a Cornerstone*:

> "Lend me the stone strength of the past
> and I will lend you
> The Wings of the future, for I have
> them."

If we solve the mysteries of the past, we might indeed discover the solution to the riddle of the future.

Dusk brings a quietness to the hills. The traffic noise is muted, the cars move slower. Out in the residential sections the crickets still sing and the fireflies glow for a second or two then die out. The surrounding hills remain more or less as they have been for centuries altering their colors only as the seasons come and go. But downtown, new structures with strange modern shapes are now boldly silhouetted against the gathering night sky. The city that for so many years seemed to stay the same, is now in a great state of change. Photo by Dick Harshaw

Southern Highlands Research Center

by Bruce S. Greenawalt, Director

The Southern Highlands Research Center collects primary sources (correspondence, diaries, papers, oral memories, and photographs) about Western North Carolina. Important among these sources are more than 22,000 photographs, negatives and glass plates depicting the region from 1890 to 1977. The largest number of these images are by professional photographers exhibiting a high degree of skill. The public may inspect and use these materials at the Southern Highlands Research Center, located in the D. Hiden Ramsey Library at the University of North Carolina at Asheville, North Carolina.

Because photographs often evolve memories and recall the past more effectively than words, they need to be regarded seriously by researchers and historians. As the photographs taken by Jacob Riis of New York tenements and factories indicate, images do more than illustrate events, actions, or places; they also interpret them. Moreover, Riis' work is indelibly etched in the minds of generations of Americans, while his writings have been largely forgotten.

Asheville has had numerous professional photographers. Among them have been Ewart M. Ball, Sr. (1894-1937), and two generations of the family following in his footsteps. Together, these men have left a visual trail of people, places and events important to the region.

The photographic records of Western North Carolina need to be uncovered, organized, preserved, and made available. The work of Lou Harshaw has awakened many of us to the possibility of photographic interpretation. The Southern Highlands Research Center is proud to have assisted her in this latest effort.

Regrettably, photographs stored under improper conditions can degrade quickly; mold, brittleness, emusion crinkling, migration of acids, continued fading, and even spontaneous explosion are possible.

The Southern Highlands Research Center offers the region a chance to store photographs under optimum conditions, and invites people in possession of old collections to donate them to the Center for preservation and future use.

The Ball Collection

E.M. Ball, Sr.

E.M. Ball, Jr. self-portrait

E.M. Ball, III. Photo by Malcolm Gamble, Asheville Citizen-Times

A great many of the old photographs in this book were taken by members of three generations of the Ball family, all of whom have their roots in the Western North Carolina region.

E.M. Ball, Sr., was born March 19, 1894 in Madison County, grew up in that area and as a young man joined the army where he served in the Philippines and during World War I was stationed in Eagle Pass, Texas. Mr. Ball started taking photographs as a hobby during the war, but soon became seriously interested in the work as a profession.

Returning from the war, he ran a studio for a while in Georgetown, South Carolina, further developing his skills.

In 1922, Ball felt the longing to return home to Asheville. He had married the former Docia Baker and they were to have three children, Ewart, Jr., Ervin and a daughter Laura Jeanette. Ball bought the Plateau Studio from Japanese photographer George Masa and it is very possible that some of the photographs were taken by this brilliant artisan.

Ball and two co-workers John Frisbee and Wayne Banks combined their skills in the operation of the studio located at 1½ Biltmore Avenue. Ball worked on a contract, shooting news photographs for *The Asheville Citizen* and *The Asheville Times* at a time when the papers employed no fulltime photographers. His work on occasion could be quite dangerous; at one point in his career he was run over by a car in trying to secure a photograph and had to spend two weeks in the hospital. At another time his life was threatened when he shot pictures of a mob trying to break into the city jail.

Ball, under constant pressure to meet newspaper deadlines, developed a new process whereby he could deliver a "wet" print in 12 minutes from the time he arrived at the studio with a news shot.

Ball also specialized in industrial-commercial work and received favorable comment from many of the country's largest industrial firms in New York, Chicago, Cincinnati and other large cities.

E.M. Ball, Sr. died at the age of 43 in August of 1937.

Ewart McKinley Ball, Jr. was destined to follow in his father's footsteps. For a while, young Ewart made photographs for the newspapers while still in high school. At the same time he was endeavoring to help his mother carry on the studio work.

Ewart, Jr., born November 22, 1918, was to spend almost all his life in photographic work. During World War II, unable to serve actively overseas due to an early physical injury, Ewart moved to Washington where he worked in a government photographic laboratory.

After the war Ewart returned to Asheville where he met and married Clara McDevitt of Walnut, North Carolina. They had one son, Ewart McKinley, III.

Ewart, Jr. was a writer as well as a photographer and served for a number of years as editor of the *Farmers Federation News Magazine*.

The most part of his professional life, however, was spent with *The Asheville Citizen-Times* as a professional news photographer. He was an active member of the Carolinas Press Photographers Association and worked constantly to upgrade photography as a profession. Many national awards were made to him for his work. Ewart, Jr. was also interested in young people who wished to become involved in the photographic profession and spent a great deal of time in working with them and demonstrating proper techniques to aspiring young photographers.

Ewart, Jr. died at the age of 47 in 1966. At the time of his death of a heart attack, he was working at what he loved best, in the studios of *The Asheville Citzen-Times*.

Ewart M. Ball, III has carried on the photgraphic tradition of this family. He worked for a while with his own studio in Biltmore Village, later returning to the position of staff photographer of *The Asheville Citizen-Times*.

Asheville has been fortunate over the years to have many fine photographers. Some of them have become nationally known. But seldom has a city had the good fortune to have preserved intact, the work of three generations of premier artisans such as the Ball family.

It was through the generous donation of the Ball Collection by Ewart, III to the Southern Highlands Research Center that we are able to present this early pictorial history. There are, of course, other important pictures from other sources, which contribute greatly to this book and they will be mentioned elsewhere.

It is impossible at this time to determine exactly which pictures were taken by which member of the Ball family, so they are designated as "The Ball Collection" in our credit lines.

We are grateful to Ewart, III and to the Southern Highlands Research Center for their permission to use these photographs.

Ewart is married to the former Rebecca Peed and they have one son, Ewart McKinley Ball, IV.

Gallery
of Pictures

Whitewater Falls, highest falls in eastern United States. Photo by Dick Harshaw

Mountain farm house and family grave yard. Photo by Lou Harshaw

French Broad River as seen from the Blue Ridge Parkway at Asheville. Photo by Dick Harshaw

Looking Glass Rock west of Asheville. Photo by Dick Harshaw

Tobacco in flower. Photo by Lou Harshaw

Rafting the Nantahala River. Photo courtesy Nantahala Outdoor Center

Nantahala Lake, highest lake in eastern United States. Photo by Lou Harshaw

Farm scene west of Asheville near Interstate Highway 40. Photo by Lou Harshaw

"Onions on the Porch" Photo by Lou Harshaw

*Nantahala Outdoor
Center. Photo by
Lou Harshaw*

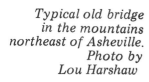

*Typical old bridge
in the mountains
northeast of Asheville.
Photo by
Lou Harshaw*

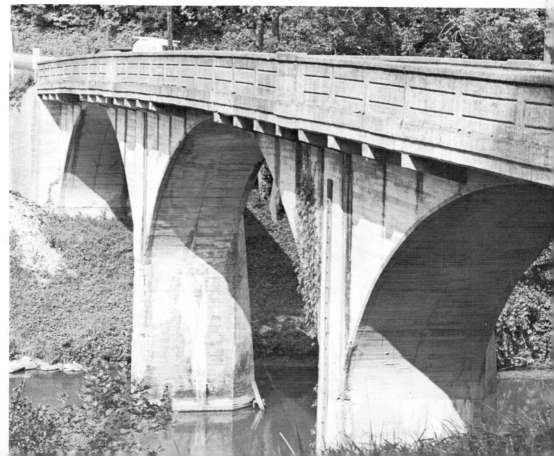

The Nantahala River. Photo by Lou Harshaw

World famous Cowee Valley in which pigeon blood red rubies are found. Photo by Lou Harshaw

A ruby mine at Cowee Valley. Photo by Lou Harshaw

*Famous "House on the Rock"
and footbridge on the Clinch-
field Railroad near Bakersville,
northeast of Asheville. Photo
by Lou Harshaw*

Bridal Veil Falls between Franklin and Highlands, North Carolina. Photo courtesy Travel and Promotion Division, N.C. Dept. of Conservation, by Clay Nolen

Looking Glass Falls Southwest of Asheville. Photo by Dick Harshaw

Modern Highway 64 near Franklin. Photo by Lou Harshaw

CATALOOCHEE SCHOOLHOUSE

Built in 1895 and formerly known as the Beech Grove School, this building served the educational needs of Cataloochee for many years. At one time as many as 75 pupils attended classes in grades o through eight. When the Park was established mos of the residents in the cove moved away, and even ally the school closed because there were not enou pupils. The last classes were held in 1958.

The old Cataloochee School-house in the Great Smoky Mountains National Park. Photo by Dick Harshaw

At work at the Oconaluftee
Indian Village (left).

Below, a scene from "Unto
These Hills," outdoor drama
at Cherokee, North Carolina.
Photos courtesy Cherokee
Historical Association

Bibliography

Books

Bartlett, John. *Bartlett's Familiar Quotations*. Boston: Little, Brown and Company, 1955 (*The Rock that Will Be a Cornerstone* by Robert Jeffers).

Blackmun, Ora. *Western North Carolina to 1880*. Boone: Appalachian Consortium Press, 1977.

Cecil, William A. *Biltmore*. Asheville: The Biltmore Company, 1976.

Champion, Myra. *The Lost World of Thomas Wolfe*. Asheville: Daniel's Graphics, 1970.

Fitts, William T. (Brig. Gen., U.S.A. Ret.). *A History of Central Methodist Church, Asheville, North Carolina*. Asheville: Central Methodist Church, 1968.

Frome, Michael. *Strangers In High Places, The Story of the Great Smoky Mountains*. Garden City: Doubleday and Company, Inc., 1966.

Langley, Joan and Wright. *Yesterday's Asheville*. Miami: E.A. Seemann Publishing, Inc., 1975

McCoy, George. *The First Presbyterian Church, Asheville, North Carolina*. Asheville: First Presbyterian Church, 1951.

Murlless, Dick and Stalling, Constance. *Hiker's Guide to The Smokies*. San Francisco: Sierra Club Books, 1973.

Sondley, F.A. *A History of Buncombe County, North Carolina*. Asheville: Advocate Printing Company, 1930.

Stanard, Wanda Engle and Carr, Emily Schuber. *Trinity Episcopal Church, Asheville, North Carolina*. Asheville: Trinity Episcopal Church, 1974.

Sweet, William Warren. *Methodism in American History*. New York: Abingdon Press, 1953.

Guidebook. *Biltmore House and Gardens*. Asheville: Biltmore House and Gardens, 1980.

Magazines

North Carolina Architect, July/August 1978, published by the North Carolina Chapter of the North American Institute of Architects.

The Magazine Antiques, April 1980, article: Biltmore in Asheville, North Carolina by Susanne Brendel-Pandich, Curator.

Newspapers

90th Anniversary Edition of the *Asheville Citizen*, July 17, 1960, published by the Asheville Citizen-Times Company

100th Anniversary Edition of the *Asheville Citzen-Times*, January 26, 1969, published by the Asheville Citizen-Times Company. Numerous miscellaneous individual articles from these two papers.

Acknowledgements

It is impossible to thank and mention the names of all those who were interested in and encouraged me in the writing of this book.

Among those who have done the most for this book are Dr. Bruce Greenawalt, former director of the Southern Highlands Research Center, at the University of North Carolina at Asheville, Mrs. Sara Folger, his assistant, and Peggy Gardner, who worked so hard and produced such beautiful prints from The Ball Collection which we were allowed to reproduce under the auspices of the Center.

Ewart M. Ball, III was gracious in working with me in the use of The Ball Collection photographs. His aunt, Larua McCormick and her husband, Harold, aided in researching the Ball family history.

Richard Thornton, Director of the Asheville Revitalization Commission, kindly gave of his time for information and later to read portions of the book and check out facts for me.

Phyllis Vance, Director of the Membership and Communications Department of the Asheville Chamber of Commerce, aided me and furnished a great deal of material.

Steven P. Miller, Director of Marketing of the Biltmore Company, has been enthusiastic not only about this book but about my other projects. Susanne Brendel-Pandich, Curator of Biltmore House, took her valuable time to check out many facts for me. Ms. Brendel-Pandich and Mr. Miller furnished me with material and rare photographs which contributed greatly to the book.

Betty Lawrence, former North Carolina Librarian at Pack Memorial Library, has over the years, offered a tremendous amount of assistance as well as have others on the staff of the Library. Many of the pictures came from their invaluable collection and were reproduced for the book by Brigid and Ralph Burns.

I am grateful that I was able to be with Mrs. Mabel Wolfe Wheaton as she talked about her family, and I want to mention Norvin C. Duncan, Director of Public Affairs, of WFBC-TV, Greenville, S.C. who gave me encouragement and assistance especially on the Wolfe portions of the book.

I would like to express my appreciation to Steve Hill, Manager of the Thomas Wolfe Memorial and to his assistant Susan Lanier.

Dr. Kermit E. Duckett of the University of Tennessee, Department of Physics, has furnished me with Wolfe material and has offered encouragement on the Wolfe section.

My thanks go to those who so graciously allowed me to quote from their works.

The sketches on the chapter facings are by Pearl Sheldrick.

I would like to especially mention my mother who has always encouraged me in the writing of the books and who has always been a staunch supporter of my efforts. She particularly wanted me to write this book since Asheville is her hometown, just as it is mine.

Sallie and Charles Thomason gave unstintingly of their time and energy, hiking miles and carrying camera equipment, but beyond that, being friends at a time when they were badly needed.

My secretary and friend, Frankie Pegg who had many occasions to lose her "cool" but never did and has never missed a deadline on this or any other of the books, deserves special mention.

I would like to thank my publisher, Ed O'Neal of Copple House Books, who put up with numerous phone calls and many questions with great patience and beyond that, offered great encouragement on the book.

Last, I would like to especially thank my husband whose sacrifices were many in order that the book might be completed. He and my son have unfailingly acted as a cheering section on the many occasions when it was necessary.

About the Author

Lou Harshaw is a native Western North Carolinian and having grown up among the rich heritage of the Southern Appalachians, considers herself a true "Mountain Woman." For many years she has been writing in a variety of ways about "this spectacular land and it's people."

Her history and travel articles have appeared in most of the large newspapers of the Eastern United States and in National Travel magazines.

Books by the author include: *The Rubies of Cowee Valley, Letters to Colleen, Wild and Wonderful, The Gold of Dahlonega* and *Trains, Trestles and Tunnels.* She co-authored with Juanita Clifton, *Reelfoot and the New Madrid Quake.*

Evermore a dedicated "teller of tales" rather than the remote historian, she endeavors to impart to her writing a feeling of her own involvement, and portrays in the unwinding thread of narrative, a real excitement about her southern mountains where time and events have created so many places of discovery.

Photograph by Davis Photographics